INTL.
THOUGHTS

ii

INTIMATE THOUGHTS

BY

Richard L. Green

www.bookstandpublishing.com

Published by
Bookstand Publishing
Morgan Hill, CA 95037
3900_3

ISBN 978-1-61863-525-9

Printed in the United States of America

Dedication

Dreams

This book is dedicated to Leslie, Gerald, Rodrey, Jeffrey, Jessica and all the children I know who have inspired me to be better than I am. It is my gift, my light shinning in the darkness showing them that in life if you are patient and steadfast dreams do come true.

Introduction

Here and Now

For the ladies, the sisters and sista's, for the friends, girlfriends, wives and mistresses of enchantments, this is the intimate thoughts of a man by a man expressing his desires, dreams and wishes. You know those small details you would like to hear and know the intimate thoughts: does he love me and how much, what does he think of me, of us?

His intimate thoughts...
Men this is a time to understand that sharing your feelings those intimate thoughts is a measure of your true emotions. It is the ultimate gift to your lady, denoting your strength and willingness to surrender your heart and its vulnerability into her hands. Thereby giving her an understanding of you, of who you are and it will answer the questions of why, simply by you expressing your intimate thoughts.

Table of Contents

Intimate Thoughts

Intimate Confessions

By Faith and Grace

Faith and Grace, Grace and Faith, Trials, Tribulations and Redemption.

It has been stated that a man's life can be recorded from birth until death.

And as part of the information recorded, we can see some of the hardships he has faced.

His trials and yes his tribulations.

However, we must not speak of trials and tribulations, without including faith and grace, grace and faith or redemption.

For in prayer we talk to the Master.

In faith we walk and by His grace we live.

It has been oft times been said that the bible is his word, the concept from which we should live.

However, as we all know man will not always adhere to its teachers, its teachings nor to its doctrine.

And there my friend is where faith and grace, grace and faith and the hand of redemption knock.

EPHESIANS 2:8 states "For by grace are ye saved through faith."

HEBREWS 11:6 states "But without faith it is impossible to please him: for he that cometh to God must believe that he is, and he is a rewarder of them that diligently seek him."

And finally:

REVELATION 3:20 states "Behold I stand at the door, and knock: if any man hear my voice, and open the door, I will come into him."

Grace, Faith, and Redemption...

A Moments Grace

A golden sunset with all its colors, a bird's flight or a mother's call.
Wake up it's your birthday; it's your birthday.
Therefore, let us reflect on life, friends, dreams, romance and love.
In life we reflect back on the decisions made and the choices presented our health and our families.
We look at where we are and hopefully plan for where we are going.
Because in life we experience the highs and lows, the good, the bad, or in other words our sunrises and sunsets
Each an experience or a part of life shared with a precious few. Our friends
You know that group of people who's always ready for the girls or boys night out.
Or that one person you call when you need to talk and just let go.
Or that select few who share those rare occasions; birthdays, holidays, silly days or those crying   days
Our laughter, fears and tears, and after the tears are shed and gone they are the ones who share our dreams.
They are the ones who share our thoughts about our dreams of exotic places, about our thoughts on romance.
They help us define happiness and are there at the fulfillment of our success and ultimately they are there when we find that special person to share our dreams.
That companion who shall redefine the concept of romance and of love.
The companion who shall show you the world through their eyes, who will let you feel the touch of a single raindrop through their senses and intimately let you experience desire, passion and the act of being desired through their eyes.
And then say! This is our moment of grace and I am yours, we are together and we are...
Life... Friends... And love...

My Cross to Bear

Scene one: A bottle of bubbles, slow groove music playing and me.
I'm reminiscing, reliving the good times. Our times…
The laughter, the smiles, the cheers…
My love, your love, our love… For a while, happiness.
Scene two: It's me again, this time with my head in my hands wondering.
Asking myself, how, and what went wrong?
Didn't I tell you enough that I loved and needed you?
Couldn't you see how I expressed my love?
Could you not understand that you are the true essence of love to me?
And now it's gone!
Your love, your smile, and your touch the last traces of a fading memory of our life.
Surely you remember? Please tell me you remember our life?
Please tell me you remember its joy's, the thrills and the trips our happiest moments together?
And yes I know you can't but remember the heartache, lies and tears.
And now that you're gone I know the depth of your despair.
I know that I am the reason for your woe, pain, and tears.
For you see, I have experienced first- hand your laughter, seen the joy and excitement in your eyes and felt the thrill of your caress.
Your love…
And now that you are no longer in my life I realize that you are my cross to bear.

A Poet "A Teller of Tales"

One night while alone, I read a book, a book about a poet called...
"A Teller of Tales"
Tales of a poet and the things he felt, his dreams, his sorrows and a tale of his first romance.
A tale of a romance that filled his heart and ruled his soul.
His first real love was in that book I read, a love inspired by a kindred feeling and the joy they shared.
A joy of times together, of walks in the moonlight, the feel of a soft gentle breeze along their cheeks, or the memory of her soft sweet lips as they kissed in the starlight.
A moment of dreaming dreams that hadn't been broken
or thinking thoughts yet unspoken.
Dreaming of things to be of thinking thoughts that come and go on silent wings and having thoughts of distant places and unfamiliar things.
The things that a poet once felt and saw that made him a teller of tales.

Shared Dreams

I think of the loneliness I feel.
Remember the joyous moments we have shared and then I wish that you were here with me sharing my dreams.
I see the sun rise upon a world lost in shadows and mystery.
The valley's touched by the sun's first light or the mountains etched boldly in their glory.
Or I watch at sunset as the land turns to darkness and slumber, preparing for a new day and I think of life.
Of how I once thought that life was so simple and easy to live and that I could accomplish my dreams, and my goals with the appropriate skills.
Or I thought that by giving my love and being loved it would hinder and impede.
That by sharing myself, my dreams or my visions the success and happiness I sought I would not achieve.
And now that I have seen the things that I have seen...
And have lived a part of life's realities it is so obvious the bad judgment I have used... Poor communication... Selfishness and sometime foolish pride...
So, what is next you ask?
Well the answers are so very simple to see.
First, I start with the act of dreaming my dreams again.
I stop pretending and hoping, and start planning and setting the goals to succeed.
Second, I look at the rules and make sure that they apply.
And finally I stop take a moment to think and ponder and ask wouldn't you like to be a part of my shared dreams?

I Am Destiny

I look out upon the land and ponder where does my destiny lie?
I sense the coming events, the hints, the whispers and the pictures.
All designed to prepare me for my destiny, and yet it only causes more confusion, more anxiety.
How can I prepare for my destiny amid this internal strife, this turmoil and this pain?
Do I continue the pretense of strength and stability?
Or do I continue to hide my true feelings?
Do I keep pushing them aside and wrapping them with a band of iron so that I am no longer vulnerable?
Or do I continue to just survive?
I look inside myself and see all of the locked away anger, the frustration, the dreams, my fears and tears.
I live with the knowledge that I am alone and lonely, and the fear that my life will always be this way.
My frustration and anger I fight daily as I deal with people circumstances and events.
Living with the hope of a new tomorrow, I see some my dreams lost or abandoned, I hide from my fears and tears enduring, hoping that someday soon things will get better.
Is this the destiny I choose? No!
Why?
Well, because I have dreamed of a time and place that shows me and gives me so much more.
Because I will find companionship, I will no longer hope but succeed and I will be at peace no more wasted tears of sorrow.
No more doubts of who I am or what's next or where do I go from here.
For you see there is only peace outside and within.
And in my dreams I am surrounded by and experiences joy.
I see the sun rise and shine upon lands that I have never seen before.
Lands that I will see...
I experience the freedom of living, of giving and sharing unlike anything before.
I experience peace of mind, of laughter and even crying. The cleansing kind...
There is no more anger, no more pain just the awareness of a time past, an awareness that I can and will experience my destiny.
An awareness that, I am destiny...

6

Redemption

I remember hearing once, someone say that the hour before dawn is the darkest part of night.

And I thought h'mm that's interesting.

Therefore, I asked myself why? And the answers, well they are...

Some say it is the blackest hour, the time of our darkest deeds, our most troublesome moments.

Some say it is the hour of walking in prayer, asking, and striving for the light of a new day.

And then there are some that say, it is just a transition period from night to day.

Me, I believe it is the hour we wake and think about our lives, and where we are.

It is the time we look back and reflect on how we have lived, and how we wish to live.

For some it is a time of revelation and change, for others despair and depression, and for the few, hope and redemption.

A time of prayer and the renewal of faith or as the old folks would say a time to go into the closet on bended knee.

A Sentimental Wish

I thought that love would never come to me.
I thought that true love I would never find only to have found love
in one such as you.
A woman of insight is special, true and sweet.
That will hold me and warm me on the cold nights to come.
Nights when I'm so afraid, alone and cold you will comfort me.
Oh what compassion I found in thee.
Such compassion I've never dreamed could be.
Just hold me and never let go.
For I'll love you for all seasons and until your last breathe blow.
I will hold you for an eternity, which can never end but go on and
on.
And I will walk with you toward a new beginning where peace is
king and love reigns.
I will walk with you each day in dawns light in a lover's paradise.
Where, our souls join in contentment, luxury and love.
I will give you my heart, I will make my heart your paradise and I
will be your dreamer, a sentimentalist or a fool.
I will be your wish so love me...

A Fond Farewell

Dreams, wishes and a reality, for as long as I can remember you have always represented each of these to me.

In my dreams I always aspired to be a person of strength just like you.

As for my wishes, well they have always been and will be that I can make you proud of me.

And the reality is that no matter how good I am or become, you will always be the model I choose to use and pursue.

Dear Mama...

I think of you even now and I smile, I think of your feisty personality outspoken ways and active lifestyle.

Or I smile at the fond memories of the things you did or gave me.

Your patience... Your love... The understanding and your time...

I remember how you always made sure that I was always okay.

How you always gave good advice about the things I did and about my life.

Your honest and matter of fact way of putting the facts so that I could see reality.

Or for those moments when I was so busy trying to be me and forgot whom you were, how the short feisty mama I knew and love would remind me.

That I am still young and learning, that I am still a child in her eyes and that I am her child.

Even though at those times it was not what I wanted to hear, or that I felt was needed I always knew that the advice stemmed from your love.

And now, that is why I want to thank you again.

I want you to know that in my heart I always tried to do the right thing.

I want you to know that because of you the small things were big things, and it was my hope to show you that you are loved in return.

It was my wish to show you that I am grateful.

For instance remember when we would disagree about how I lived my life or the things I was doing and it seemed as if I wasn't listening and a couple of hours later or a day later I came to you and said I loved you.

Well I was, I heard every word and felt the emotion and the pain.

The only thing was that I needed to be independent; I needed to show my willfulness, and still have my dignity and pride.

Remember I am your child and for me you have always been strong, willful and unchanging.

I have always thought of you as home, my refuge from the world at large because I always knew that your arms and door was always open for me.

I always knew that you would welcome me back home; however on this journey I now take I must walk alone.

So! Until that moment when I will welcome you in my arms again, I bid you a fond farewell.

I love you now and always.

A Mama's Joy

I look back on the yesterdays of her life and see the dreams she cherished, the hope she nourished come to naught because of the constant changes, pain and strife.

She! My mother would speak of the life she had lived and endured, of her parents and growing childhood.

In the hope of teaching us to learn, to live life to its fullest and maybe hoping to one day to be understood.

I can hear her voice speaking to me of her dreams and fears, of her hope of a brighter tomorrow, her laughter and her tears.

Of her childhood she spoke with such longing of things past and gone.

The values!

Of her family, when she spoke you could hear and feel.

The pride!

And oh! When she spoke of her children you could see the light of love upon her face.

Ah! I can see the images, as they appear of a smiling child full of joy, a young lady blooming into womanhood and then as a mother experiencing life maternal pleasure.

And then I remember how she spoke with such sorrow of the things she missed, of the places unvisited and her inner yearnings.

Of the small regrets of a time and place that could not be recaptured.

The put aside childhood dream of the White Knight in shining armor, in order to face reality.

And then, I can see this aura; this light begins to shine from within her as she smile and say to me;

Baby it was worth it.

For you see, for all the years she lived, for all the talking and teaching she did, she believes there is no greater dream to achieve than A Mama's Joy.

A Prayer of Thanks

This silent prayer I ask of thee.

That as I walk through life's trials, that you see me safely thru.

When I'm sick and discouraged, your spirit fills me bringing comfort.

Or in times of doubt, give me the understanding of thine word its binding message and joy.

Or when I am alone and confuse I ask that you spread thine healing hands and hold me.

Oh father I ask that you keep me in thine mercy, thine grace in your glory and your power.

Father I thank you for thine blessings and honor you with this my silent prayer of thanks.

An Everlasting Moment

In the days of old in a time gone by, a time of brave knights,
fiery dragons and those searchers of adventure.
I journeyed the world over in search of a sign, a sign
of great possibilities.
A sign that promised all dreams to come true, fame, wealth
and the dream of all dreams an everlasting romance.
Long ago, in the city of stars I saw this vision flash
across the skies.
A vision of a place, a time and a moment my destiny revealed in a
soft, soft cry.
A cry as light as a whisper and yet louder than the
beat of my heart.
For in this cry I felt the longing for love, the need
for a gentle touch, and the desire of life.
The desire to find joy and happiness, to soar upon the
winds of time and to experience an everlasting moment.
A moment of sharing with a friend, of dreaming dreams
or a moment to listen in solitude and peace.

Beyond Tomorrow

I was once told that dreams are the windows that show us our tomorrows.

They are the bridge that connects our past with the here and now, our present.

Dreams... dreams...

My dreams, beyond tomorrow...

First I look back and review relive and rethink some of my actions from the past.

I look at the pain I feel now, have felt and that I have caused.

Then for a moment in time I pause and ask myself the question; is this where I want to be, is this the person who I choose to be and where do I go from here?

Now it's like I'm stuck that moment in time has become more than a pause and... and... finally I find an answer that's not an answer and it is, to refocus, dream again and look beyond tomorrow.

So I sit down with paper and pen to start my journey.

I outline the areas of my life in order of importance and then I begin. Faith... family... companionship...

Faith... how do I describe to you faith? For me it is the very air I breathe and is in every fiber of my being.

Faith, it is now and always will be my foundation.

Family... like faith when I speak of or think of family I fall short of the proper words and the only thing that comes to mind is unconditional.

That is unconditional love, unconditional support, and understanding.

You see unconditional will help family understand what it means to you when you look past the here and now, and when you look past the yesterdays of yesterday and dream.

And in most cases unconditional will allow them to share in your dream.

Faith... Family...Faith, family and beyond tomorrow...

So today I think of the memories I've made alone and those shared. Companionship...

I think of the plans I've made, we've made our talks and dreams of what was and could have been, what is and what would be.

So many times you spoke of the walls I put up to block out the world and you, or so you thought.

I tried in so many ways to let you in to see through my eyes that I needed and wanted you, I tried in more ways than one to let you know that no matter what picture I presented to the world you always had the original live and in person.

Commitment... Do you remember the first time that I said I loved you and my reaction?

From that moment on I changed little by little, for me in ways I didn't understand I got better, felt stronger.

In other words I was committed to commitment... and I was in love.

I think about the poems I have written or read; in my eyes, in the moment of desire, seduction, when I'm with you, you are, I am destiny, and timeless memories, and then I think of my life faith, family, companionship... love, honor, commitment... and for me I have no other choice than to look beyond tomorrow.

By Your Side

I look back on the yesterdays of my life, and think of the questions asked or the answers given and realize that they are no longer important.

Still, when I think about the decisions made or the choices presented I must say that I don't know where the road may lead.

Because, you see I find myself searching the people around me, listening for a voice I have never heard.

Yet knowing inside that this voice, of this person will soon be mine.

Her thoughts I will know from a glimpse of her eyes, the passion she feels her warm embrace.

I will know her from the scent of her and her aura.

And I will allow her embrace to wrap me, to fulfill me and satisfy this yearning within me.

And I will experience visions of my dreams that will turn into reality and that will allow me to realize and hold my pot of gold at the rainbow's end.

A reality that will allow me to live the joys of life whatever they may be by your side.

Cry A Tear For Me

I was once told that in life everything has its season.

In the spring the birds sing and love is in the air, there's new growth in the flowers, grass and trees.

In the summer we feel the sun and see the effect as it brings to full bloom all of the growing things.

Again, the season change preparing us for fall, a time of wonder when nature sheds her vibrant colors for the softer tones and a time of rest as we drift into winter.

Dear mama I look back at the life we've had and I want to say thanks and also that I love you.

I here have been so many things that I would like to have said but didn't, that I would like to have done with you and for you; unfortunately our time has been cut short.

Therefore I will tell you now the things I would like to have told you before this moment.

And that is for me you are and have been the greatest mother a child could wish for.

I would like to have told you that because of you there was never a moment in my life where I felt alone or unloved.

Because I know that no matter what the circumstances, you were only a call away.

There were so many times that I just thought about you and smiled.

So many times when just the thought of you kept me, when the thought of you sheltered me and when the thought of you made me realize that you are and have been the first act and final chapter of my life.

Therefore as you read this, my last thoughts and wishes please remember me as I was with a smile on my face, laughter in my heart and with you on my mind.

My mother... My friend...

My mother, my friend, my heart and if by chance you have to cry then do so.

I only ask that if you must then let them be the cleansing kind.

That if you must let them be the healing kind.

And finally if you must, cry your tears and remember me with a smile!

Desire

H'mm, I look upon your face and smile.
Think of you, your look, your voice and feel my desire.
I see the sunlight shine upon you in its golden splendor.
Hear the wind blow whispering your name and still do I feel my desire.
For you see when I look into your eyes I yearn to hold you forever.
It is my wish then to give you my heart's desire.
It is my wish
to give you unconditional love full of trust and devotion, compassion, understanding and passion.
It is an unconditional love where you are my queen, my dream and my one true love.
Desire!
How can one word express that which I feel when I kiss your sweet lips?
Can it fully express the raging emotions inside as I hold you in my arms?
No!
Does it or will it quench the hunger I feel as I look into your eyes?
Or will it conquer my fears of one day not being by your side?
No!
Then how can I express to you this single word desire?
Simply by saying this... I stand poised upon the edge of an abyss, trembling, remembering, yearning and when I see or think of you.
I fall!
This to me is desire.

Emotions

Gently ever so gently do I dream of holding you near.
While whispering softly to you, my laments of love.
Your sweet tender lips, could I kiss?
Your soft smooth skin I would dare to caress.
Never did I say life with me would be a bed of roses.
Yet we have each tasted of its pleasure and smelled its fragrance.
Like a rose each act of life has unfolded, blossoming from first bud to full bloom.
Memorable times we have shared that shall remain in my heart.
Memorable acts I shall remember in times of sorrow in hopes of a smile.
Or when I hear your voice I smile, look into your eyes the emotions come welling up inside.
Then there are the times when the thoughts come unbidden, and I need to feel the embrace of your arms.
While you whisper softly of the changing emotions inside and tell me; we can never be just friends.

I Will Remember

Lord I come before you this day asking of thine comfort and wisdom, because I know that you are a just god who has infinite wisdom, understanding and love.

Therefore I come to you humbly in my hour of need seeking thine mercy for my mourning heart.

I come to you seeking healing for my worn body and tired spirit.

And finally lord I come seeking you my everlasting father so that I may have access to the tree of life and join you and my son in our heavenly home.

Amen…

Lord I know that you have all power and infinite wisdom and sometime there are things that happen and it's not meant for us to understand.

But as a mother, a father lord I got to ask. Why my baby?

I got to ask couldn't you have given me just a little more time?

Oh lord, forgive me!

I know that I shouldn't question your will, your judgment.

It's only that all I can see or remember is his smile.

I walk into each room and there is a moment when I expect to see or hear him.

There's a moment when I think of holding him dreaming of his future and mine.

I can close my eyes and picture his big bright eyes and beautiful smile.

I can draw a picture of his actions the awareness he showed in people and the things around him.

Or I can tell you about the way my heart glowed with love and pride just watching him grow.

How I would smile at the silly faces or expressions he made.

Or how my heart jumped with fright when he fell or something went wrong.

Or should I tell you that as of this moment my heart is so very heavy.

That my heart longs to hold him once more, that my heart longs to feel his hand in mine and that I just want to see him smile.

Oh lord, help me!

I just want to touch him once more and know that he's all right.

I just want him to know that I love him and that I will always remember.

In My Eyes

My dear lady I am writing you this poem to express to you, my dreams, my adoration and my commitment to you.

First I would like to say that I love you and in more ways than I can say that I need you here, near always.

There are times when I sit and think about my life and where I'm at and the thought of you pops up in my mind and I smile.

I see my dreams of what I want and where I want to be and see you standing there beside me and then I realize that love shows and time heals.

You see I always said that for me love was a onetime deal, for me after all of the heartache and pain had faded and healed that, that was it for me.

No more

But then after getting to know you, spending time with you and seeing what true love is and what it has to give.

I realized that it was useless of me to pretend or to say otherwise other than that you are my heart's desire.

Simply spoken I love you... Desire you... Want you... Need you... And will have you now and always...

So I am asking you to try and understand that I will make some mistakes and more than likely I will make you very angry at times.

However please remember that you are the one that makes me smile at the thought of you, you are the one that makes me smile when I see you walk your stride and you are the one who makes me smile when the weight of the world presses me down.

Please remember that love heals all of the hidden pain, fears and doubts, that love heals because true love well it has no bounds, and that is unconditional and uncontainable.

And finally I ask you to understand that for me you are now and always have been the spark that has fueled my inspiration, the hope that I choose to believe in when I think of my dreams and aspirations, and that for me well you are simply.

It... You are...

In The Moment of Desire

For a moment if you would, just stop and think about this sentence.
In the moment of desire…
For some I can imagine that you know exactly what it means, and for those who don't let me explain.
So listen carefully.
There are times, moments in time when I long to hear your voice, see you smile and long for your embrace.
My body, mind and soul ache for your presence, your touch, your scent and taste.
Desire… At that moment I'm in the moment.
Then there are times, moments that I cry, filled with such joy, such ecstasy that words seem inadequate to describe my feelings for you at that moment.
Or there are times, so many times when the moments are shared and our eyes meet when our souls become fluid and our love, our purpose, our destiny is without question.
It simply is, and at that moment we definitely are in the moment.
And then there are times, moments when the teardrops fall one after the other and my heart is ripped, aching, for the shields and walls have risen and I'm lost in a tangled web of words and actions I don't understand.
You see I think of how you make me feel, your touch, and your smile.
I think back to the things you have said and how you say it and the only thing I can do is relive that moment and smile.
And, at that moment I'm in the moment of desire…
At that moment I can put aside the times when I want to run, run to escape the pain of those times you flee so far away inside yourself.
At those moments I can put aside the doubts, the fears, and the loneliness that beckons me to withdraw and retreat, for I am still in the moment of desire.
Desire… Desire… Desire…
There are times, many times, more moments than I can count when I cannot escape.
I cry and smile simultaneously, simply overwhelmed by my feelings and emotions, mesmerized by the love I feel for you, by my desire to be here fully and completely for you.
And yes at that moment I am in the moment, and without question, it simply is…

It's Time

How can I say always that which I feel?
Each moment with you the emotions are stronger more heartfelt.
Simply spoken, I love you is not enough.
As time passes each thought of you and the time-shared rushes upon me.
Or that longing for those promises envisioned within my mind daunts me.
Or I question myself seeking answers I do not have.
Therefore I embrace the joys of life waiting to see if it is our time.

Loneliness

Sitting here, thinking of you and the times we've shared.
I can't help but wonder wills the days to come be for us as happy or as sad.
Happy I say to myself, yet knowing, as the teardrops fall that it is only a lie.
Still, I remember the dreams and how when you spoke your eyes held mine.
Each knowing from a glance, that we were meant for the other to share life's pleasures,
And also its pain...
Looking back on those years and the times we've shared, I can't help but feel the loneliness
As I sit here alone.
Each moment, an eternity filled with the silence of an empty home.
The silence I feel when I'm alone, thinking my thoughts of you.

Losing You

I now see why in time they say the pain fades.
Still, as I remember those moments we shared my heart yearns and I wish.
Oh, how blind so very blind was I not to know true love I had found.
Yes, had found... For you see I realized to late my mistakes.
Now all that remains are the memories we shared.
And each day as the time apart lengthens; I slowly fade from your life.
Or when I hear your voice I know that I'm losing you.

Memories of A Child

Dear Mama
I think of the things you taught me, us your children.
Or I remember the love you gave to me your child, and through remembering I feel the comfort of your spirit and your love.
I think of the things you did when I was a child and it makes me smile sometime, then at others I cry.
I smile at the pictures of us, our times together shopping, laughing and having fun.
Or I remember how you would read to me and act out the characters, you with the big eyes and the silly faces.
My mother the teacher, the actress my friend...
I smile at the memories of you being proud of me, my first step, the first word I spoke, school then college and now.
Do you remember your smile as I walk across the stage at graduation time?
And like you I can still feel the tears and remember how it felt when off and away from home I went.
I can still feel the tears as I struggled with life and the hardships over the years.
And then I think of the things we spoke of or I think about how you would face the problems we had when I was a child and my tears dry up and I smile.
You see I remember the things you taught yet didn't teach, the stories you told without speaking, the strength you showed without flaunting it.
And at that moment my smile gets bigger, my heart feels stronger and my love well it will always be seen through a child's eyes.
I will always see you as strong and smart.
I will always know you as the problem solver you are.
And in this life you are and have been my mother, my father and the love of my life.
You are the tower of my strength and inspiration, my shield and comforter.
My teacher and friend, you are loved.

28

My Change of Seasons

It is now winter and the leaves have turned.
For me it would seem as if our time apart has been a lifetime ago.
Yet, in reality it has only been a very short period of time however, the essence of you still lingers.
The sound of your voice and your touch...
The memory of who you are, the way you smiled, you walked, you talked.
Or that special way that you moved your head, your hands or how you stood.
Physically I desire you, for what you are and because of my belief in you.
It makes me want to be a part of your life; I want to know that when you smile I am the reason.
Because you remember my passion and you have just had a thought of me.
I wish to know that when you laugh I am the echo of the reason.
The reverberation of a thought you have remembered about a moment of our time together.
And if by chance you cry, your tears are my tears the reflection of the hurt I hold inside.
And when you cry, it flows from me to you then away.
Because, you are my essence and I am your essence and together we are sharing.
Two hearts beating together in rhythm with one beat.
Once not long ago it seems I had these thoughts of this beautiful dream.
Of you and I together building a life, growing closer, and being each other change of season.

My Cross to Bear

Scene one: A bottle of bubbles, slow groove music playing and me.
I'm reminiscing, reliving the good times. Our times...
The laughter, the smiles, the cheers...
My love, your love, our love... For a while, happiness.
Scene two: It's me again, this time with my head in my hands wondering.
Asking myself, how, and what went wrong?
Didn't I tell you enough that I loved and needed you?
Couldn't you see how I expressed my love?
Could you not understand that you are the true essence of love to me?
And now it's gone!
Your love, your smile, and your touch the last traces of a fading memory of our life.
Surely you remember? Please tell me you remember our life?
Please tell me you remember its joy's, the thrills and the trips our happiest moments together?
And yes I know you can't but remember the heartache, lies and tears.
And now that you're gone I know the depth of your despair.
I know that I am the reason for your woe, pain, and tears.
You see, I have experienced firsthand your laughter, seen the joy and excitement in your eyes and felt the thrill of your caress. Your love...
And now that you are no longer in my life I realize that you are my cross to bear.

My Final Goodbye

My smile, your smile, our smile...
Candlelight... Starlight... Moonlight... Daylight and night night...
Now close your eyes and think, I have enjoyed these things and so much more with you.
I can remember the trips together, the movies, our talks, and the dreams you spoke of.
For me, the way you spoke captivated my interest and my heart, it made me want to be a part of your life, your dreams.
It made me think that I was important enough to you and that you wanted me to share and experience you.
Your success and failures.
I remember smiling at myself and thinking I'm in love.
Or, I saw you again walking towards me and it was as if it were my very first time seeing you.
Your beauty, your walk that look... The way you made me feel, the excitement.
I stood taller because I was standing next to you.
I became stronger hoping that one day I could be that shoulder you needed to lean on or that friendly ear when you wanted to vent and just let go.
Your wants and desires.
I can think of the moments, our moments together, it brings a smile to my face, and I tingle inside.
Or I remember each day moment by moment, each minute multiplied.
Each hour prolonged and I am desperately awaiting your return.
So I may express to you again, my love for you. My joy in you and my pride...
So that I can tell you once more that you are and have been my friend, my lover and my conscience.
And that you are the best part of me, and this is my final goodbye...

My Journey's End

For me it started the moment I first saw your face.

At that moment you had me in the moment of desire.

I wanted you by my side always and in my dreams of success you where the person who I envisioned at my side.

The person who I could tell my deepest secrets, my fears, the one person who I felt could understand me, my heart, and my soul.

I believed that I had someone who could understand that with a little time and patience our goals and dreams we could achieve.

Yes, I said we could achieve... Together.

You see in my eyes I could see the dream turn into reality.

I could see the picture expand from one panoramic snapshot to a full three dimensional view.

Our journey's end...

So I took the first step we talked, I listened, you listened, and we planned and spoke of our past, the yesterdays, our today and our tomorrows.

We dreamed separately and we dreamed together.

Always it seemed as if no matter how much we stumbled or had to adjust the reality of what we shared survived.

For me that was enough, I knew that you loved me, I knew that I loved you enough to be patient and at times to be as understanding as I could or as understanding as the moment allowed.

Always hoping that someday you would do the same.

Always hoping that for you; at some point the things I did or didn't do would show you what my heart truly felt.

I hoped that by never leaving your side and always being there in your time of need and even when you didn't need me you could see my love for you and know that you are...

My MIA amore', my change of seasons, my mocha surprise and the tears I've cried.

You see for me it started the moment I first saw your face and now at this moment I realize that I'm at my journey's end.

I realize that for us we are at our journey's end...

My Love

As I think of when we first met I smile.
I remember the words you spoke and how your eyes held mine.
Do you remember my love?
You said we were not supposed to meet and I said we were.
To me it was divine.
That sense of belonging, the familiarity, the closeness and that sense of being fulfilled.
I remember how when we first kissed I longed for it to never end and I whispered I love you.
Do you remember?
Never did I dream that love could be so sweet, or that I would want to give all of myself my heart, my soul.
A prelude to a promise of a lifetime and that is that I will love you for always.
I tell you this now because, I love you and becauseyou are my love.

My Mia Amore'

A solitary flower...Your dimples... Your eyes...

My Mia amore' this is for you, for the times I didn't say or didn't have the words to express how I felt.

For the times I held you in my arms and smelled your fragrance thinking of how you complete me.

Or when I lay beside you thinking and dreaming of the future and what it holds in store for us.

And finally for the times I've said or wanted to say I love you but didn't.

I will say it now and hopefully you will understand what I truly mean when I say I love you...

Therefore, with that thought on my mind I will now explain to you these feelings of mine.

Stop! For a moment and think back to when we first met and remember the words of what I said.

Now listen to what I'm about to say.

For as long as I can remember I've dreamed of finding that someone special who would love and accept me.

I've dreamed of finding that special someone who I would want to give myself to unconditionally.

I've dreamed of loving that person with an abandonment that would inspire tears of pleasure for no reason.

That would inspire laughter just because.

And that would heat my passion so it would never cease to burn hot at the thought of her, hotter when I glimpsed her and it would become a raging inferno ready to consume her when I feel her touch.

Your touch... you see in reality I'm talking about you, my dream realized.

There's not a moment of the day that if I think of you I don't smile, or if things get kind of rough I close my eyes and picture your face to hear your voice and see you smile

Because, to me you are the calm amidst all of my everyday storms.

You are my friend, my lover and the very essence of my heart.

My Mia amore'... you complete me.

For the longest of times I would always keep the feelings I had locked away and bottled inside.

And then. You walked into my life like a ray of sunshine on a cloudy day and from that moment I have been a different man.

34

From that moment I grew enough to be able to tell you the things I feel and fear.
From that moment I could open up and tell you that you are my Mia amore' the love of my life.

My Sorrows

I look back at the yesterdays of my life and think of how time has passed me by.
Of the dreams I have lived and achieved.
And I smile to see a part of my life etched so bold and clear.
My concepts, its clarity and yes also its purity.
Then I think of those dreams that have faded or the ones I lost along the way.
And they remind me of a sunset and its colors.
It reminds me of how the colors fade into the coming shadows shifting, fading and how they blend into each other never to be seen again only to be thought of in rare moments.
It's like a reminiscence of the past known but forgotten.
It is impressive, yet it is still only shadows of a time of growing, of dreaming and of striving to achieve success in life's realities.
It is a time of facing our fears our shadows and its different images.
A time of learning and finally acknowledging who and what we desire to be.
They are our dreams our shadows and my sorrows.

Our Moment in Time

I reminisce on my dreams of yesterday; you know my desires, my wants and the hope of a better tomorrow.

Or I remember the plans you spoke of, about you and I.

Plans that included a nice home, maybe some traveling to exotic places some entertaining and growing old together.

Don't you remember the fifty years I spoke of?

About watching the kids grow and living their own lives.

About my thoughts on being a grandparent and my get even plans by moving in with the kids.

Or the smiles we shared at the thought of spoiling the grandkids, or of you rolling me around in my wheelchair.

Fancy that, you got to admit the thought is tempting.

You see I think of the promises we each made, the commitment we both have shown and given, and I know that growing old with you would be more than an everyday adventure.

For me it would be true happiness.

It would be our chance to express and experience love in its truest form.

Our chance at sharing a love that is uninhibited and unparalleled.

It is Humble, unconditional and all encompassing

It is my anchor in life's tossing seas and my shelter through the raging storms.

It is the foundation of my strength and security, the spring from which I drink knowing that our love is:

Fulfilling...

Adaptable...

And understanding...

And, that's how I know that somewhere, somehow we will someday have our moment in time.

Out of the Night (A Voice)

Listen! Did you hear it?
That voice out of the night from an age gone by, from a memory out
of my past.
Did you hear it that whisper out of the night to haunt me.
That soothing soft silky voice filled with promises of
happiness and excitement.
Yet it's only a facade, a terrible dream.
There it is again, that voice, why does it haunt me so?
Can it be the girl of my dreams calling out to me?
Calling out of the night, where is she? I must know!
Oh lonely voice, guide me to thine master.
For only she can free me from this voice, out of the night.
That fills me with such longing for her touch, her embrace.
Hold me this whisper say's love me and make me yours
for all time.
While we sail away on an ocean tide to an island of paradise.
From out of the night a voice spoke these words to me.
Cheer up my brave knight in shining armor for someday
I shall soon return.

Seduction

A brief glance, a smile, your smile, that smile you know the one with the seductive smirk and the down turned eyes.

Yeah that's the one; come on girl let me seduce you.

First I walk across the room, you know smooth and slow.

Then I step to you, all the while making eye contact and looking into your soft sexy eyes.

Thinking... Thinking... Damn! She's fine.

Then I stop, gather my thoughts and say hi.

You respond back and the conversation start.

We talk about our likes and dislikes, the small things.

Advance to the big things, all the time still maintaining that electrifying eye contact.

And then we smile, together and speak about our wants and desires.

You know the things that turn us on.

Like when I stand up and pull you close, while looking at you and you ask me what?

Why are you looking at me like that?

And I answer because! As I walk a slow circle around you getting closer and closer.

Then I stop directly behind you; you can feel my breath on your neck, my body heat upon your back.

My presence... and then I lean a little forward and brush my lips across your neck and lightly caress your arm with the tips of my fingers and then stop, lean back and moan, hmmm!

Let me seduce you, hmmm, can I seduce you, hmmm, will you let me seduce you?

Now I take a step closer until your body touches mine and I place my one hand across your stomach and my lips next to your ear and ask; can I, will you, let me, seduce you, right here, right now?

And your answer in reply is a soft... soft...soft... sigh.

So I tighten my arms around you and pull you close, then closer until you are wrapped in my embrace.

Then with a gentle grind of my hips I mold my body to yours, and I caress your body with mine.

All the time asking are you ready to be seduced, can I will you let me, seduce you? Can you feel my desire?

And this time you answer with a moan of desire.

So I pull you closer and grind a little harder, a little stronger and run my hands ooh!

Smile for Me

I hear the laughter in your voice as we talk.
See the smile upon your face when I look at you.
Or I can feel myself falling as I look into your eyes.
Their depths I could explore for all eternity, languishing
in their warmth, their color as their beauty astounds and mesmerizes
me.
I fall and the enchantment is broken only by the softest touch of
your hand across my brow.
It is broken by the whispery touch of your lips upon mine and the
glimpse of your face as you teasingly whisper my name and say
smile for me.
Then I close my eyes and think of how when I hold you in my arms
how my heart races as does the clouds across the sky.
And how I can feel you there beside me, my anchor in the tossing
storm.
And then I smile and turn to you and ask will you smile for me?

Stormy Weather

Blow oh storm and let thine forces free and rain
Won't thine fierce winds blow this tumult in my heart away
across endless skies
While yet my tears fall from thine stormy clouds
On let not my anguish darken the skies as would a storm
To make thine fierce winds howl and blow with a ferocity as
does my heart
Lighting, oh jagged lighting which lights the darken skies as
does her smile lights up my life
Oh thine magnificent and enchanting thunder which rumbles
across the heavens
Yet reminds me of her lovely laughter so soft and true
Stormy weather let not thine fierce winds blow the memory of
her from my mind
For as a tree may bend from the ferocity of a strong wind
so my love will I
My love for you is as a very strong foundation that
cannot be changed by any stormy weather.

Sweet Passion

I mourn the moments we have lost.
The sweet passion we shared, the ecstasy and the tender silence.
Sweet passion is what I remember when I think of you.
Your touch I still feel when I close my eyes.
Your voice I hear in the silence as I walk through my empty home.
And then I lay my head upon my pillow and I smell you!
Your fragrance and again I think of your sweet passion.
The way you smiled when I held you in my arms.
Of how your body responded to mine as I lay beside you.
I hear your laughter of joy as we sat and talked.
Or the soft moan of desire as I kissed your neck, your arms, and then your lips.
Your oh so soft lips their sweetness I still taste.
And now that you are gone I hear this voice inside of me whispering, no shouting!
Passion, passion and that you were my sweet passion and that I was yours.

Tenderly Yours

My dear lady what must I do? What can I say?
This love for you is ripping me apart
Oh how I wish you could truly understand this
feeling I have
A feeling of many hurts, yet soothed by a memory
of her touch
Memories of her sweet kisses, her soft gentle
caress and our moonlight talks
Talks of days to come or of lonely days gone by
Lonely days spent thinking and dreaming about
your beauty
Days thinking of a paradise of a perfect love
Days of calling you on the telephone talking,
whispering tenderly across the miles, then ending
 it by saying I love you, good-bye
Tenderly yours.

That Smile

Ah, today I have beheld a sight as I have rarely seen.
For a blossoming flower shown before my eyes, a flower
in the form of an enchanting smile.
A smile so charming that it filled my heart with excitement.
Excitement as I have never known, yet have longed and wished for.
But, now to have it within my power is so very much like a dream.
A dream that slowly builds toward a shattering climax, or a
fantasy filled with romance.
Romance with a picture of you, your eyes, your face and lovely
hands but most of all, that gorgeous unforgettable smile.

The Choice

Each day at sunrise we greet new life.
While dawns light shine upon a world awakening from its slumber and softly lights each shadow as man rises from his dreams preparing for a new day.
Still the night visions linger, taunting, whispering of choices yet to be made.
Choices containing truth of character, wisdom gained and knowledge of times past.
A gift of life for each man decreed by god but decided by their choice.

The Strength Within

We have talked on several occasions about people and their values, of how we each must face our daily battles not with our physical powers, nor with a vocabulary filled with words of distinction big or small.

But from the inner strength we have within....

For you see I stand accused of so many things and most do not matter.

They are the lies of the idle minds, and the petty thoughts of the weak and envious.

They are the people who don't know that self esteem and beauty shines from within.

Still it pains me to know that human nature can be so corrupt, so uncaring and blind to the beauty of life.

Our Choices....

For you see I believe that each person is inherently good and that we each have a choice in how we live and how we wish to be.

The egos should not matter, nor the power perceived or imagined.

Only the strength within...

Through The Years

While seeing some of the joys of life I think back on those memories of yesterday.

Wondering, which were better those from the years before or those of today?

Today, I say aloud are definitely better but, then I feel the whisper and stirring of my heart.

Or I remember the thrill of the romance I experienced or the all so carefree manner of the cultured gentleman in his elegance.

Then I must say that those from the years before are better, only to change my mind when the vision of you crosses my eyes.

A vision of you maturing day by day through the years experiencing all that life has to offer with a smile.

The Tears I've Cried

Knock, Knock, Knock… Ring, Ring, Ring… Still no answer…
Picture this, candlelight flickering throughout the room.
Soft romantic music playing in the background and you're all-alone.
Sounds familiar…
Now close your eyes and I'll draw a picture of a time and place filled with the tears I've cried.
Once upon a time not so long ago were I was bursting with pride and uncontainable hope.
That's right, you guessed it that magical word. Love…
You know that kind that's not supposed to be measured in bits and pieces or that's not supposed to come and go.
Nor is it the kind you feel at the height of pleasure or intimate bliss.
But, the kind you can hold onto, or better yet you know the kind that holds onto you.
In romance it would be the single tear that one perfect rose.
In prose or verse a poet would write and speak in terms of beauty, the depth of color and love.
Therefore, let's start verse one intro.
A poet a dreamer of dreams am I still dreaming and writing the tales of my life.
There was a time when I thought true love I had found.
You know, the sweaty palms, the nervousness and the goofy smile.
I remember thinking each time I walked into a room and saw you damn! She's mine.
Or… When you looked up and saw me watching, how you smiled your dimples and your eyes.
Even now I can feel the touch of your breath as you whisper you love me.
I can close my eyes and envision your spirit intertwining with mine.
The memories… The smiles… The pride… Our feelings.
The walks… The talks… The laughter… Our sharing.
The intimacy… The pleasure… The understanding… Our giving.
And now, nothing no light, no love only the tears I've cried.

Time

Oh time won't thy be still?
Still my heart for to endure another day without her is agony
Time slow down and let the minutes drag by and let thine hands go
back in the past.
While I remember and think of the beauty of her face
Let thine hands go back in the past.
For how can I live without her in the future?
When the things we shared are only mine, for I can remember at
last.
I can remember my love for her so precious and true.
That time itself cannot outlast or endure.
Oh so much, yet so little time to share.
For what mortal soul can out age father time
None, none! Oh agony, agony! Why must life be so hard?
Oh time won't thy stand fast?
For this most precious moment must linger and last.
It must oh time come to me allow me a moment more because life
is so unexcited and lonely.
For time thou has changed me. Why? Why!
I am so alone and sad with only memories to cheer me.
Like time my life is slowly passing away
And all that shall be left behind is a thought, a memory.
Time won't thy stand still for me?
Then I'll have a chance to leave something behind my legacy.

Timeless Memories

Today…I think of my childhood and smile at the memories.

I close my eyes and see my life, a picture that holds so many vivid reflections and recollections.

I see my family, my friends and our lives I remember the Sunday dinners after church, the ball games, and school.

I can remember dreaming about who and what I wanted to be and hearing my mom say; you can do anything and be whatever you want if you set your mind to it.

And look at me now, a country boy now living and writing a part of his dreams, telling the world about his inspirations and aspirations.

Look at me now a country boy showing the world the people who inspire his life. His heroes…

My mother… Always a lady, forever strong… Always understanding and indispensable…

She is my mother, my friend, and my hero! Loveable… Funny… And inspiring.

You see I reflect back on our life and remember how she managed the pain, tolls and strife and I stand taller.

Or I think about the sacrifices she made for me, us her children and I then think of my love for her and realize that for me it can never truly express what I feel for her, this lady, my mother.

Or I reflect back upon the actions of my father, his wisdom, his strength and the sense of stability he gives.

He is a gentleman in its truest form, a scholar, honorable, a teacher and a protector.

Think for a moment if you would of a man who would give his all to allay the fears of his child, or that would strive with all his might to try and satisfy their wants and desires.

This man is a father, my father… He is the foundation of my pride, my honor, and my strength. He is my hero!

For a moment if you would think back to your childhood.

The dreams you had of conquering the world, of being strong and smart just like dad, or beautiful and loveable just like mom.

Remember how she held you that time when you hurt yourself and came to her crying, or that time she blew softly on your finger when it hurt for no reason.

Or the times your dad, my dad listened to you talk about what you did or accomplished, and after you were finished he gave you a hug or patted your head.

And all you could do was smile, because, you could feel the love, the pride and at that moment your world was complete.

No fears, no doubts, no worries. Just happiness like now as you think of your timeless memories.

Unspoken

What should I do when I can't say the things I feel?
Do I hold them inside and hope that you understand or feel the same?
Or should I just say I love you and hope that you read between the lines?
Tell me, how can I explain to you the emptiness I feel inside?
How can I explain to you the hunger for love and acceptance that only you can give when I'm in your arms.
The expression I see upon your face the joy, the happiness and the surprise.
Do I wait until I see you and look into your eyes or hold your hand and wish with all my heart that your love is as strong as mine?
Tell me! Oh tell me!
What do I do when the fear and loneliness makes me tremble inside?
Do I hold it inside and fight the fears or just let it all go and cry my tears?
Tell me, what can I say to make you understand the joy I feel when you are near?
The fear when you are gone? Or the intense pleasure of your touch?
An expression filled with tenderness, longing, and the need for love.
Tell me, will this love I dream of be a love of a lifetime or just some time we have shared.

When I'm with you

Once not long ago you asked, if I would write something for you.
I remember thinking yes, however, I did not reply.
Until now...
I could write about the stars, the moon, the sun and how beautiful they are or how the wind stir the flowers, the trees.
Instead I will write about you, my hidden thought, that sudden smile.
You know the reason I have aspirations and inspirations.
Or when I'm with you how I stand taller filled with pride.
Or our times together shared in silence yet, we each know that the other is near and that we are never alone.
Or sometime when we look at each other we both see that hidden wonder in the other's eyes.
And either you or I will ask what? What are you thinking and then just smile?
Stop, and for a moment listen to me as I close my eyes and draw you a picture of what I see and feel inside.
First I see the aura that surrounds you all sparkly and bright.
To me, it is simply beautiful.
Second your face, your smile, both enchanting and an enticement to open my eyes.
However, there is still a picture left of you of how you make me feel.
How when I'm with you everything is and feels right, or when I hold you in my arms my world is complete.
I have no worries, my troubles of the day just falls away and all that I can think of is sharing this moment and being with you.
My Mia, you are my hidden thought and sudden smile.

Why Should I Say Goodbye

So, tell me.
How do I tell the woman I love goodbye?
When I remember all of the things we have shared; our walks, our talks, the way
We have embraced and made love.
Or do I speak of the changes I've made in becoming a better man?
Do I speak of the ways I express myself when I tell you how I feel?
Or the number of times each day that I say I love you, while holding you in my arms.
Then there are those moments when the mood is right and I feel the rush of emotions and I know that you are my heart's desire.
It is at that moment when I know that you are the one person who can share all of my dreams and wishes.
The one person who understands how I feel and what I need.
So tell me, how do I say goodbye?
Do I forget about the past we have shared and look toward the future and someone else?
Or can I still dream of the future we envisioned and talked of?
Tell me baby, how do I say goodbye?
I look at the times coming and I'm filled with dismay.
I think of the talks we've had and my heart yearns for the softness of your touch.
Your warm embrace, and your voice whispering to me the words I love you.
Please don't go!

Wishes

I look back upon the dreams we envisioned and I wish.

Or I think back to how the rapture felt and I smile.

Then there are the moments of remembrance and only now do I see all of the possibilities we had.

Only now do I realize the dream was within my reach, and that you were my vision, my reality, my life.

Somehow as time moved along reality changed and each value crumbled within my grasp and I changed.

Still, I look back upon the deeds done and think to myself if only I had known.

For you see each lingering thought speaks to me and tells me it should have been you.

Yet as time passes the reality that's it's over haunts me and all I can say is that I wish things had been different.

You Are

If I could think back to a time when I could close my eyes and not see your face.
Then I would say I'm forgetting.
Or… When I walk into a room, look into your eyes, and feel the nervous jumpy feeling inside.
What must I say other than I love you?
So… It is now time for me to tell you, you are my heart's desire.
I can close my eyes and see your face, your smile.
Think of the moments we've shared and hear the laughter in your voice; the caring, the love.
Or when we embrace and I hold you close I feel the closeness of our thoughts.
The beating of our hearts together and the voice inside of me screaming, yelling.
You are!
I can stand in an open field with the sun shining upon me, yet when I'm near you the heat is greater.
Or I can feel the wind blowing, see the breeze among the trees and yet your touch, your caress to me is gentler.
Therefore… If I could write a poem in verse or prose to say the things I yearn the most it would say that I love you, I miss you and that you are forever my heart's desire.

The World Without

It is a grandiose scene that reminds me of the world without.
It is from the outside looking in lively and full of color, fun and exciting.
It is mine and yet it is illusion.
For I am voiceless. It is illusion for I am invisible... I am untold... And therefore unsung...
So teach to me a song and I will sing to you my praises.
Teach me how to write and I will create songs for the world of the histories of our people, the facts and the fictions.
Teach me... Teach me how to write and I will compose a line that will speak volumes and call to souls.
I will compose sentences that will turn heads, freeze brain cells and make your body two step to the words in motion.
They will be sizzling hot...
I will write a poet's tales and a writer's dreams a scorcher...
It will be sweltering like summer in the south, steamy like an exotic trip to the jungle or like passion long denied. Erotic... Mythical... Fulfilling... Orgasmic...
Teach me... So teach me the adjectives I will need to describe to you my thoughts of the world without.
Teach me and I will describe to you a world filled with the wonders of nature its beauty.
I will describe to you a world unfeeling at times and yet at others compassionate. It is Erratic... It is changeable... And it is misleading...
It is the world without with a purpose within.
A world where I will be the visionary that describes to you what a blind man sees upon his first sight. It will be awesome... Devine...
I will be that hallucinogenic vision the addict see's of paradise at his most intense high. Fantastic... Unsubstantiated... Quixotic...
For I am man born of dust plucked from the heavens fallen to a world without where I am neither outside nor within.
And yet I will rise to the heights of a utopians dream and I shall be perfection.
I shall rise back to the heavens from which I came and be perfection.
I shall rise upon an angels wings and stand before my God upon his throne who is perfection and I will ask father am I worthy. I will ask father will you speak to me... Will you teach me...?

58

And his reply will be to take me into his arms and show me the visions he has planned for me.

His answer will be to hold me in his arms and with his touch the images flood my mind and I can hear him speak telling me that I am born of him and in his image.

His answer will be to hold me closer and then release me back to the world with a final message that states perfection is earned through trial and error and for me to learn.

His answer will be that perfection is earned when I have mastered the lessons and for me to learn.

His answer will be to return me back to the world with a fading image that tells me that man is born to strife and that with each breath, that with each heartbeat I must learn to understand.

That in this world those who are in it can sometimes be without, and sometimes those who are without can also be within it and that life is worth the journey. The tears… The laughter… The smiles…

It tells us that sharing visions and believing in dreams of perfection is simple because, the world without beckons and perfection is perfection.

Through The Storm

I am Alpha the first born, the first son, life's first breath and dawns first light.

I am the birth of a nation the harbinger of life and I am Adam born of dust the first man.

And I am love for I am Eve born of bone taken out of man, companion to Adam I am the first woman!

I am love, I am temptation and I am desire, together we are hope, emotion, pain, pleasure, passion, and redemption.

Together we are a lesson for we are the fallen.

We are fear, we are loss, a devourer and death for within us we hold the darkest night and together we are Omega the broken swords walking in darkness eternal and like dust motes we are dancing through the storm.

John 14:6 "Jesus said unto him am I the way the truth and the life; no man cometh unto the father but by me."

Spiritually I stand between two doors one open and the other closed torn between what I see and the possibility of what may be.

You see as I stand between the doors the things I have been taught wars within me I see the beauty of the earthly things, feel the excitement its action and at that point I am a worldly man.

I am a worldly man that wants the action without consequences, the excitement without restraints and truly no conscience.

However that second door reminds me of; the what ifs, it reminds me that life is much more than the excitement without the restraints and the actions without consequences and I remember that life without a conscience is full of pitfalls where we trip and fall and fall and keep on falling.

That second door reminds me of prayer and of the possibilities that it can accomplish and of the doors it can and does open.

It reminds me of the fact that there is always more to life than just what we see, than what we know or have learned, it reminds me that the experiences in life that we feel, that we touch or those that touch us are infinitely small and that they are life's lessons.

Whereas emotionally it reminds me of that old song titled "My Life Story where the first line begins with the words I've had my share of life's ups and downs but fates been kind and the downs have been few."

And like that song I guess you would say that emotionally I have had my share of shocks that have reverberated through me from end to end, I have had my share of heartbreak, my share of lost love, my share of wanting and needing to feel that I am worthy.

I have had my share of falls not knowing if I had the strength to get up and try again yet trusting in faith and believing that I would.

For through the tears, the laughter, the loss of loved ones, and the aloneness and the fears I have stood on faith, I have fallen on faith and risen.

While intimately I speak to my God in prayer, I speak to him in conversations where we speak of the dreams I have, my ambitions... I speak to him of the aloneness I feel and he tells me that I am a part of him and that no matter where I am he feels me that no matter what I do he feels me and no matter how I speak he feels the intimacy of my words their depth, their meaning.

And then he tells me that through it all he will hold my hand through the essence of time then hold me until the last star falls and time cease to exist.

For he is Alpha and Omega the first and the last all powerful for he is God.

Together

Practically I sit and think of the lives I have lived and of the people I have touched and I am amazed.

I am stunned by the implications of the things I see and by the logical conclusions of the things I think.

Some days as I revolve around the interior of my mind I stumble upon a path of memory that is shaded and shadowed.

I stumble upon this path and the few steps I take show me that life is an infinite wheel that turns continuous and that we are but motes flying into its flames.

Figuratively I can describe to you the innermost thoughts of whom and what I am inside. But I won't...

I could use flowery words big adjectives and adverbs to tell you the things that I would want you to know about me. But I won't...

You see life has taught me that, no! The journey along this shaded and shadowed path has taught me that the things most important should be learned on our own and not just simply told.

I have learned that the things that are heartfelt last longer and are stronger.

Respect... Love... Admiration... Desire... Compassion... Happiness...

You see life has taught me that alone the spark I make is dimmer that alone the spark sputters.

In all sincerity I will say to you that with all of my flaws I am better with you.

I will say that with you by my side the unfiltered is filtered and the unbiased becomes biased and the hundred percent is purer and more genuine.

I will say that the once heard you are a good person is more believable.

The once heard you have a good heart is more acceptable.

The once heard you care about people is no longer something to smile at but can be embraced.

It can be believed... Accepted...With you it is truth... And I am real...

Candidly I shall talk to you about my wants and your desires.

I will tell you of my dreams and listen to you talk about yours,smile at your enthusiasm, laugh at your intensity and cheer you on.

I will hear you ... Feel you... And hold you not once, not twice but until eternities end and beyond... Because what we share transcends time and span eons, it is authentic and unparalleled.

I will say that although you say that I am your strength that you are mine.

I will say that although you say that I am your rock that you are mine.

I will say that although you say that I am your wisdom, your friend, and your lover again I will say you are mine. Mine... Mine...

I will say that there are moments when your eyes beseech mine and our thoughts tangle and I am mystified by the emotions I feel.

And that sometimes when we rise beyond the clouds and cast the fetters from our minds together we are greater.

I will say that together we shall shine like the stars distant and dazzling, burn hotter than the sun and walk gracefully hand in hand.

And although it may seem that our journey together has been destined and that our destiny has been ordained, I will say that I wish to rise and fall with you, love and cry with you and know that together we are forever inspired.

An Island of Stone (Symbolizes a Heart)

I once heard of an island, an island made of stone.
It was told in this tale that it was the stone of lost ships from days of old.
Days of old when the wind howled and the seas raged an all encompassing rage from the deep depths within.
Up from the depths of darkness came the chill of the unknown of a sea gone wild with rage.
It was the elements unleashed in all of its fury as waves and wind against man.
It was nature against the men of the sea and the land beyond.
Each wave pounding with the wind howling in its fury at a land of prosperity and success, washing away at the broken hills and rolling forest.
While along the beaches lie the hulls of ships past.
Hulls of ships washed ashore from an angry sea.
A sea of beauty and serenity which can all change
Change adventure to fear or an island from sand to an island of stone.
It is the changes that slowly built from the wrecks of ships of old and the memories of today.
Memories of love lost or days of cold hearts to come of
days when people just won't care and hearts turn cold
Cold heartless people, people who have a heart of stone.

I Miss You

I miss you like the desert miss rain
A rain which holds my life in check
Oh if only you could come back to me
For I miss you, your wisdom and kindness; but, most of all you
Come back to me and then I will say I need you
For what can I do without you to guide me
Oh come back, come back! I need you, I miss you.

The Ringing of Bells

Only to hear a tinkle, a chime or that sweet thrilling sound from the
ringing of bells
While looking out my window upon the world, and remembering
your laughter
So like a soft bell a sound of beauty coming from the heart
A pulse of sound that adds serenity and gives a sense of mellowness
That effortlessly drifts upon the edge of the mind, while slowly
gathering into a harmonic melody
A melody that softly sinks to the depths within, igniting a flame of
fire and passion that will
never cease to burn
A spark burning within and sustaining the misty light which
gleamed intensely out of her eyes
Only to gather and explode into a moment of ecstasy where she
heard the ringing of the bells.

The Star of India

When the breeze softly blows and the clouds part look for the symbol
a star over a quarter moon.
It is the star and moon that shall be our guide upon this wintry night.
It will be our guide to a golden treasure or to a new beginning that few have seen and many dream of.
Bear upon the star and follow its silvery light across the glistening waters.
As thine eyes fall upon a glorious scene that I will chase over the world
by following a quarter moon.
Ah! What adventures and dangers may we encounter upon this journey.
in search of lost kingdoms, filled with silver and gold.
While our hearts cry out in vain for understanding and for romance.
The romance of a lifetime brought upon an unsuspecting heart while in search of happiness from the star of India

A People's Pride

As I look back over the years, I see all the struggles and hardship my people have had
I see the many roads they have travelled in order to uphold their pride
Then I look at my people today and see that the struggle is still present, no more no less
But when I think about the trials we faced, the pain endured, then I must salute my people's pride
The revelations of each act done; from the beginning of life or until life departs
Each generation a step ahead steadily, slowly marching onward
Destined to pursue and ever illusive dream

I Now See

As I remember our time together I now see all my reasons for the
things I did.
Blinded me to what was right.
Such as, my dedication to you and my desire to commitment to you
and lastly for the things left unsaid for those things untold.
Because now I see honor forsaken, brings ruin one can't avoid.
Still if one but holds to the promises made and cast away the lies.
The love will grow.

A Majestic View

Ah to see such beauty cast across the skies.
Such colors that flashes and glimmers then slowly fade into twilight.
Only to rush back upon the mind in more splendor than before
the reddish tinge so very much like blood itself.
Or that pinkish tinge cast upon the clouds from a dying sun
only to be lost in the enveloping folds of darkness.
Darkness that creeps slowly along, slowly brushing aside
and erasing the colors of a magnificent sunset.

A Tribute to Love

I imagine this moment… But no… No…It's real.

So real… I listen to the emptiness around me and think of what once was; how you made our home seem alive, the smell of cooking in the air, the scent of your perfume and you.

I think back to a time and place when the concept of me falling in love getting married being happy and complete was unimaginable. To some…

And then I met you and it seemed as if my step got lighter, my mojo was better and I was smiling.

Smiling and in love… Smiling and walking down the aisle… Smiling and just now realizing that for seven years you have been my wife, my lover and my friend.

For seven years you have been the shoulder I leaned on, the backbone that held me up and the water that quenched my thirst. For seven years…

As I think of our memoirs, our legacy and our memories I wish to tell you again that I miss you… That you completed me… And that when my tears come unbidden in the midnight hours you alone comforted me…

That I think of you always… That as I stand here in this moment in time and remember our life I feel the pain of your passing, miss the feel of your touch, the sound of your voice and I miss knowing that you are home waiting for me.

They say that a man's life is changed when he has someone who needs and wants him. It makes him stronger…

I say a man's life is the decisions he makes, the people who are in his life, the responsibility he accepts and his ability to rise from the many falls he takes in life. As I imagine the same would apply for a woman also although, most time I only hear the expression that; a woman is defined by her family, her children, her husband and lastly by her own personal pain and suffering.

By the strength she gets from the tears she cries… Her faith… and her love…

Once long ago I may possibly have agreed however as I stand here looking within this moment, I see that the true measure of a man is made greater by the woman at his side.

And that true love once found transcends all boundaries lifts all burdens and change lives.

I wanted to tell you that your love made a difference in the man I am now versus the one that I was and that I am faithfully yours and this is my tribute to our love.

A Love of My Own

You once asked do I love you and am I in love with you.
And I answered as I always do evasively; I remember my reply as being you know I do and left it at that.
Your next question was how much and again my answer was vague and evasive.
It was that I have never found love that could be measured by its weight or volume or by its width.
I have found that love, just is.
Therefore, I will answer the questions you asked of me, and explain to you the depth of my love for you.
Do I love you? Simply spoken; yes.
Am I in love with you? Yes.
Can I prove to you my love? Honestly, I don't know.
I can talk to you of how I feel my wants, my desires, my goals, dreams and tears.
Emotionally, I can speak of how you make me feel, the silly smile, and nervousness inside, the sense of security and strength you give, along with the knowledge that the shadow of your love encompasses and surrounds me always, simple and unconditional.
Mentally, I can think of all the reasons that I love you or I should love you.
The emotional highs I experience when I'm with or around you.
The peace, the comfort I feel the happiness the love you give.
And physically, well let's just say I crave your touch, and how you touch me. The way you hold me in your arms is mine alone, and late in the midnight hours when I'm awake and alone the thought of you, your voice, your body is so compelling and arousing.
The thought of you at that moment makes me want you then and there, completely, absolutely for always.
It tells me at that moment that you are my love and that I have found the love of my own.

My Life's Flow

I once looked within the mirror of time and saw a mirrored image of my life's flow. From a single look I saw the constant twists and turns, the hesitation and the instant decisions.

I saw… And then within a moments breath the image changed and I was only looking within a mirror.

Sometimes there are days as I open my eyes I can recapture a glimpse of moments gone or those yet to come.

I see a happier me remember a happier us and long for a happier tomorrow. Sometime… Then there are moments when it seems as if from the past comes a voice tolling the bells of times gone reciting the litany of our moments shared and our feelings.

It tolls and the vibrations of what I feel, you feel or what I have felt, or you have felt resonates within me for I am attuned to only you.

From within me comes a voice telling the tales of my life, the tales of our lives, it tells of the thoughts I have as I look at what and who you are, it tells of the thoughts I have as I think of how we are together our feelings.

Everything, from how I look at you to your response, everything from my knowing that I love you, that I am in love with you to the fact that this is how love is supposed to be magical.

It is supposed to be and feel like a clear bright sunny day dazzling.

And sometimes it is supposed to rain so that the water nourishes and replenishes our soul so that we can journey to the rainbows end and talk about the answers of life, our desires to grow old together, or the desire to search for the answers of life and to experience them along the way together.

You see there will be moments when we don't have all the answers and we may have to bend but not break, cry to cleanse our eyes and sit silently when we would like to shout.

Or sometime when the nights are long and the mood is right we shall embrace and hold each other until dawn's light.

Or for those times when our trials are hard and our days are dark we shall talk of our troubles, remember the smiles and pray together through the darkest part of life.

Behold I dream of standing upon the mountaintop of time reading the pages of my life.

Remembering my dreams of what I thought my life would be.

Reviewing my actions and the results thereof the ever widening ripples of my life's flow.

74

And then I awoke to the image of reality and I realized that life is simply a circle that turns, a wheel of infinite possibility and the pictures we see and live our simply snapshots of the scenery.

Another Birthday Has Come

Today I aged one more year
A year filled with waiting and hope
Waiting for that magic nineteen
While, yet hoping that things will remain the same
In heart, mind and my feelings toward my fellow men
Men who live on the verge or hysterics, yet those hearts are filled
with compassion and love
Oh, on this special day let not us forget where we came from
So we can maybe understand where we are going

Happy Birthday

Hope this day is filled with cheer
More so than all the other days in this year
Even though I'm not there to help celebrate this special time
I say and wish you a very merry and truly happy birthday
So smile and enjoy thy self for today is thine, for the doors of wisdom are slowly opening to you
Opening and revealing a world of prosperity and joy
A world that has been laid at your feet, a world to be taken on your birthday
Joy be unto thee

My Sunrise

Hearts fire the journey
Once again I come to you asking that you close your eyes and visualize this scene for me.
It is approximately 6:00 o'clock a.m. The sun is about to come up and you are waiting for that perfect sunrise.
You have your morning brew in hand, reminiscing on better days.
Sunrise... At last now I'm fully awake thinking of you.
How I miss the sound of your voice because it is music to my heart.
How I miss seeing your face and looking into your eyes hoping to catch a glimpse of your soul.
Or how I miss the way you look at me. Hold me as I feel your heartbeat against my face when I place my head on my special place. Or how I miss knowing how your day was and wondering if I could have made it better.
I remember each moment and hope that I won't miss another chance to know better you or to become closer to you.
You see just one glimpse, one word; one kiss from you brings a great deal of joy to my day.
Because... It is you and only you that makes me smile.
Smile, its sunrise and I'm thinking of you.
I'm wondering if I could write this poem to express to you the things I've learned.
Wondering If I could write this poem so that it would say to you exactly the things I feel and need it to say.
Such as; you are my sunrise the light that shines and makes the darkness of my life brighter.
The candle which burns a never ending flame and the rain that falls upon my dry parched soul. My sunrise.
The star that shines even brighter before me and I long greatly for your to fall and make my wish a reality.
For you are my hearts fire, my sunrise and the start of my journey.
Because smile, I'm thinking of you!

Through This Pain and Suffering

Through this pain and suffering I have found myself
Found myself to be a person of many moods and changes
Moods of temperament and changes filled with depression
Depression of the mind from day to day
While, yet my heart wants to burst from within
Burst from lack of joy, burst from this pain and suffering
Oh, just let me hold your hand once more to experience reality
Reality of a life filled with happiness and joy
A reality which takes away the pain, the suffering and gives one joy

INTIMATE
CONFESSIONS

Dedication

To my mother Essie and father Jim Green, my brothers and to my sisters, this is for you for the countless number of times you reserved judgment and just believed. For the love you expressed endlessly and for being my foundation. I always know where home is and no matter how the road twists and turns it will always lead me home.

The Foggy Mirror

Reflections...Reminiscent...And Poetic...
To live in the present is real
To show the past is but once was
Smoke and shadows is all you see
For neither is real
Accept that fall as a lousy hand of cards
Focus on prayer for the why questions.

Knowledge... Wisdom... and understanding...
To understand is to believe
The past is what has been
The present is what is
And tomorrow is but a dream of what may be
So focus on prayer for the direction you wish to go
Accept the why questions as a lousy hand of cards and toss them to
the side.

Acceptable...Fallible... And inspiring...
For man to achieve he must first dream
Some will say that he must learn from the past
For the road he chooses to walk have an infinite number of
branches
Prayer will direct his steps
The past will show the mistakes of those before
And the present will be the mirror from which he sees himself
For understanding and acceptance man must first be willing to fall
Otherwise his life is a lousy hand of cards that he can never toss
away.

Vanity...And responsibility...
To look upon his life man must first open his eyes
For the mirror he seeks lies within himself
Vain is his belief that life owes him
Truth is in prayer
Understanding is in his questions
And acceptance is holding onto that lousy hand of cards to play
them another day

I Don't Understand

Slowly, slowly I order my thoughts.
I slow my breathing and channel the urge to lash out and to attack.

I breathe in and then I exhale now I'm ready. To teach... to listen ... and to understand...

Think I am the teacher who stands alone teaching concepts that no one wants to hear.

I am the teacher who provides the ear to listen for those who need to talk when the world is deaf to the voice they cry out with.

And I am the well from which the answers flow, the pillar for the leaning shoulder, and for those souls who are forever searching then I am the lodestone that is forever shining beaconing them on to their dream desires.

I am the teacher a dream maker, an idea builder, and a bringer of hope to the hopeless.

I am a poet...

Slowly, slowly I order my thoughts and listen to what I've been thinking.

I can hear my thoughts revolving around, the ideas of life.

I can hear my thoughts bouncing around inside of my head and I pause with pen in hand waiting for my thoughts to flow.

Waiting, waiting, waiting... Slowly my thoughts form and I listen as the words begin to flow.

I can hear the rhythm and the rhyme of the words as they transcend their original meaning.

I can feel the depth of the words and see the vision that they inspire.

And I hear the resonance of the words as they echo across this room hopefully bringing enlightenment and understanding.

I hear... I can hear... I have heard the words spoken and still I long to understand. Poetry...

Think I am the poet who writes about the concepts of life.

Such as; Love... Relationships... Trust... Honor... and Our Dreams...

I put into words the brief glimpses of life that I see.

I put into words the sounds of life that I hear and that I feel.

To share with you my ideas my feelings and my thoughts, while baring to you the very essence of my soul.

Think I am the poet who writes words and phrases that enslaves the mind.

Think I am the poet who writes words of wisdom that inspire the intellect to achieve the unknown.

I am the poet that writes the words that have you saying that was deep, hmm or I don't understand.

I am the poet that writes... I am the poet that inspires... I am the poet that teaches concepts most have forgotten, concepts most don't understand.

I am a poet and hopefully you understand.

The Message Within The Lines

Today… I dreamed of my yesterdays, my today and my tomorrows yet to come.

I sat and thought about the good times I've had, the mistakes I've made and my fantasies.

And then I think of the many times I've spoken the words if I could have.

The many times I've wanted to explain me the man, the mystery behind the lines but didn't.

You see I have given the world a picture to view that shows the best and worst times of my life.

I have given the world an unbiased view of my innermost thoughts, dreams and the visions I see and embrace.

I have shown the world the pain that I hold inside to remind me of what once was.

Along with the tears I have cried and those that I still cry.

You know, those tears that remind us that life is still good and forever changing.

Or… Sometimes it's those tears you cry to just release the pressure, the distress, or those just because tears.

Those just because I'm tired tears…

The just because I'm alone tears…

And you know just because there is no rhyme or reason it just happens…

Today at this moment I took this moment to analyze my life.

88

I searched the innermost recess of my heart and mind and found that my heart is lonely.

That I'm still yearning for acceptance...For love...And for understanding...

I found that by looking inside at this moment in time the mystery of who and what I am has changed.

I found that I still have so much more to give in terms of trust, of wisdom, and of love.

I found that by taking this moment in time the mystery has been revealed and the message is written within the lines.

Today... I dreamed...

If I Could

Turmoil... If I could explain to you the action and choices for my life then you would believe. In hope...

If I could show you the tiniest glimmer of the light from which I work from then you would understand. My tears...

If I could write in prose or verse effectively to say that which I long too tell you then you would know. Of love...

If I could hold you and you only for forever and feel your heart beating next to mine then I could say that for me. That would be heaven and my greatest happiness...

Or: if I could look into your eyes until our souls flowed together as one, kissed you until the very essence of time stood still.

Then and only then would I say that I am complete and that you are my reality...

Wishful Thinking... If I could take the sun, the moon, and the stars and mix them into an elixir then you would know how high you make me. Yes you...

If I could show you, tell you or explain to you how the sight of you and the touch of your hand laid gently upon my arm, my shoulder, my chest stirs me then you would realize that you are; my heart's desire...

If I could define the word desire to my satisfaction to you, then the world would stare in awe and bow before you. But the reality is.

My words, my actions, the explanations and definitions are not enough nor can they ever be enough to show you the true picture of how and what I feel for you.

The reality is that if I could have shown you the world. I would have...

The reality is that if I could have said that I am yours. I have and I did...

The reality is that if I could have said that I love you. I have many times...

The reality is that I simply want to give you, and show you all that I am.

I want to illuminate the darkness around me to show you that here I am. I'm yours forever...

So if I could have said goodbye. I never would have...

And if I could have told you, shown you or convinced you otherwise. Then I should have.

With My Eyes Open

One word... Daughter...

Definition; you are the reasons that I smile, the unconditional in love and the reason that I stand taller, walk straighter and show my pride.

Daughter... One word yet it has so much meaning and it gives such understanding that it is more than one word.

Daughter it is a word that inspires a mother or a father to protect.

Daughter it is a word that weaves a spell of changing from rules to smiles to tears.

She is a catalyst that can spark a revolution, can enrage a mob or inspire a nation. My Daughter...

Behold one word with so many possible revelations.

To me she is all that a daughter should be kind, loyal, obedient, honest and loveable.

To others she is what the moment desires or the needs be.

And to herself she is herself strong, faithful, consistent, and a realist.

She is a dreamer with an attitude, and has a confident smile that lights the darkness around her.

She is a pillar of strength for the tired and weary.

A fountain of joy for those who love her, in fact she is truth, she is trust, and she is love.

And me I'm a father looking at her with my eyes open.

Timeless Wonders

They say that in life there are eight great wonders, however for me there is only one. You...

I have read of and seen the Tower of Pisa, Mount Rushmore, The Sphinx and the Egyptian Pyramids and the others.

I've watched this world spin from satellite views and dined in and on terraces from city to city, and from coast to coast.

Felt the burning sand upon my feet as I walked the many beaches, tasted the salt spray upon my lips from these world oceans.

I have flown the skies and seen the sunsets and sunrises in all of their many shades and colors.

However, you are still the greatest timeless wonder to me.

You see I have watched you live your day to day life and it still amazes me that no matter how much I have learned you still teach me more.

I'm amazed that as you grow older the wisdom you gain is so much more apparent.

I'm amazed that as I hear you speak of the past and the trials you have faced that your strength of character is still strong.

And that no matter how many times I come to you, the advice you give is always heartfelt.

And I know that it has been tested, tried and proven.

I have watched you weather the disappointments in life and keep on smiling.

And when I asked you how you could just accept things as they are or how they were given?

Your answer was, that time and patience heals all…

That time and patience heals all…

Time and patience heals all…

Hmmm… I have watched you age gracefully… seen you walk in your pride and with dignity… tried your patience and love…

And no matter how many times you have been tested, I have never found you lacking and to me you are the greatest timeless wonder of all.

The Soul of Poetry

One wish... Two kisses...And a dance under the stars...

Moonlight... Teardrops... and a silent serenade of your favorite song...

Memories... memoirs... and a faded image from a snapshot of the past...

Once not long ago I spoke of love in all of its elegance.

I spoke of holding you close and whispering the desires of my heart to you.

Of telling you that you are the one who my heart desires... The one...

Three words, here I am and an Eternity with a wish to show you the world in all of its flavors...

Our western traditions... my Southern hospitality... The Northern impressions... and the Eastern mystic revelations...

Some day... One day... Today...

One word! Poetry...

It is one of many visions of what life is or can be.

One word! Poetry...

It is the Inspiration that can inspire and does inspire.

It is the inspiration that changes things and people.

It is one word! Poetry...

Poetry...Poetry... Poetry... Poetry!

It is the soul of all that is or can be.

It is the sound of the things that we feel...

It is the color of the things that we see...

And it is the heat in our passion the caress in our touch.

It is fire in our desire the fuel in our words... Our thoughts... And our actions...

It is love, sorrow, understanding and confusion.

Poetry... It is soulful, revealing, and Poetic. Poetry...

Four words; The Soul of Poetry a pen some paper and a story to be told of what once was, is or can be.

Three hours three minutes and three seconds later the story is complete.

Two words... I am...

One word! Poetry...

The Way I See Myself

You may look at me and see that I am not smiling and say that I am not happy.

You may hear the tiredness in my voice and see the way my eyes flutter with weariness and say that I am not taking care of myself.

Or sometimes in my moments of deepest regrets or despair you may see me wipe the tears from my eyes and say that I am too emotional.

Or you may look at how I look, the way that I talk, how I dress or the way that I walk and say that I don't fit your normal profile.

And then I would say, you don't know me and that is your perception.

You see I am more than a happy smile with a perky attitude.

I am more than that one or two moments in time where I cry my tears and wipe my eyes.

And the tiredness well, think of it like this I am tired because I am capable of doing.

I can do, am doing and will continue to do all of the things that you can't do, will not do and those things that you have no idea of how to do.

Because I am me, and what you see is what you get.

I have a face bearded at times and then at others it is smooth shaven…

My hair is trimmed and barbered, can be in dreads, curls or twists…

And my nails are trimmed…

My shirts are pressed and my pants are tailored to fit…

I am soft spoken with a vocabulary...

And yes I am a man, strong yet silent, bold with an attitude and at other times I'm shy...

I am myself...

I am a brown skin brother who is three shades of black.

Face... hands... and butt...

Face sun aged browned to a mahogany tan...

Hands two shades of black one side dipped in mahogany and full of flavor...

The other side dipped in a pail of sensuous flowing honey...

And my butt well, let's just say that it is all of the colors of my inheritance, the reds... browns... tans... yellows... and black...

It is the Dark Continent brought to life...

It is the final shade of midnight...

And I am myself... so if you don't like what you see then...

Well...

The Road I Have Walked

Some of you will look at the picture you see of my life and smile. Some will look at me and wonder, what is so unique or special about me? And then move on. Envious speculation...

For some I will be that flicker of light within the darkness seen but elusive. Hope...

For others I will be the reflection within the mirror, their reality. Life...

For the select, select few who have gotten the chance to see and know me the man. Richard...

Who, will say that I'm okay. Because...

They have gotten the chance to see me smile... hear me laugh... or just take it all in...

They have heard me speak about my children... my family... my faith... my poetry...

And for the very, very select few who have gone the distance with me and beyond.

They have gotten the chance to feel and experience my love.

They have gotten the chance to see the inner me.

For some it has brought enlightenment and intrigue...

For others it has caused confusion and disappointment...

You see a light shines brighter in a darkened room more so than in the sunlight.

And the road I've walked has been filled with the obstacles of life and still is.

I've stumbled more times than I can count.

Cried, cursed, pleaded, begged and promised myself that if!!! Things got better I would change.

And like you when things got better I forgot. Temporary insanity…

You see I rode that wave of illusion like a surfer rides his waves I was smooth.

I shifted and swayed to each motion, bent and flexed with the board. I was it…

I was bigger than life and on top of the world. My greatest illusion…

In simple words I am a simple man, the possibilities I express are unlimited, my potential is beyond measure.

However, reality still reigns supreme.

And again I am just a man, not a myth nor a legend.

I am just human…

Showing you my reality and a small section of the road I've walked.

The Heritage of Prayer

Heavenly father…

We pray for your anointing grace, that the lines that separate us bring us closer together. And that the hungry get fed, the insecure find security in you and that the bottom level be risen up to the top in Jesus name.

Written by Andre' W. Matthews

My Lord I come unto you asking for courage… wisdom… knowledge… and understanding…

Written by Mariquita Lopez

Once, long ago, I was told that thru prayer we commune with god so that he may know our hearts desires.

Therefore when we pray, we pray for thanksgiving and in thanks.

We call out to him for his divine blessings and forgiveness.

Like, Mariquita, when I pray, I ask for courage, wisdom, knowledge, and understanding.

Then, I pray for the endurance to finish the race we are running and the life we are living.

The Courage to face the truth about the answers we seek and the ability to grow from them.

Knowledge… So that we gain enlightenment on this path we tread called life and so that we know what we know.

And understanding… to interpret the knowledge we have gained and use it according to god's will.

So that with the wisdom gained we can use the knowledge, understanding and courage wisely.

For we have all heard that, "the race is not always won by the swift but by he who endures to the end".

So therefore if we pray diligently, and be steadfast in our commitment to god then the covenant that he promised is now our heritage.

Thru prayer, we commune with god, asking him... seeking him... and finding him in faith as we pray.

Now, for a moment, please kneel with me.

Heavenly father...

I humble myself before you seeking your grace, asking that you keep on keeping me, that you keep on protecting me and that as I call upon your holy name by my faith you shelter me within your ever loving arms. In the name of Jesus.

Amen...

Hearts Fire the Journey

Once again I come to you asking that you close your eyes and visualize this scene for me.
It is 6:00 o'clock a.m. the sun is about to come up and you're waiting for that perfect sunrise.

You have your morning brew in hand waiting, reminiscing on better days.

Thinking, sunrise at last now I'm fully awake thinking of you.

Of how I miss the sound of your voice because it is music to my heart.

How I miss seeing your face and looking into your eyes hoping to catch a glimpse of your soul.

Or how I miss the way you look at me, and hold me close as I feel your heartbeat against my face when I place my head upon my special place.

Or how I miss knowing how your day was and wondering if I could have made it better.

All the while hoping that, I will not miss another moment of getting to know you or of becoming closer to you.

You see just one glimpse, one word; one kiss from you brings a great deal of joy to my day.

Because: for me it is you and only you.

Smile its sunrise, and I'm thinking of you.

I'm wondering if I can write this poem to express to you the things I've learned.

I'm wondering if I can write this poem so that it will say to you exactly the things I feel and need it to say.

I'm wondering if my words in prose will express to you the magnificence of the term you are my sunrise, or what I mean when I say that you are the light that shine and makes the darkness of my life brighter.

Or, that you are the candle, which burns a never ending flame and the rain which falls upon my dry parched soul.

And that you are the star that shines ever brighter before me, my sunrise, and my inspiration.

You are... you are... you are... and yes you should smile because I'm thinking of you.

It's you

When I think of you it's like my world shifts and I fall.
However, the funny thing about it is that no matter how many times I fall there is never a painful landing.
And for that I love you...
I could list the many ways in which I fall.
Or I could tell you that you are my moon and my stars.
However, that wouldn't be as effective as me saying that I love you...
That I am yours...
That you are mine...
Or that it's you...
So when I speak of falling for me it's a good thing.
Almost like summertime when it is all hot outside and you order your favorite shake then drink it really fast and your brain freeze for a moment.
Well... the only difference is that instead of my favorite shake it's you.
And instead of my brain freezing for a moment it smiles and expands, and then I can feel the tiny explosions of my brain cells pop like soap bubbles blown upon the wind.
Drifting...
And again I can feel my world shift and like before I fall.
So I close my eyes and call out to you risking all that I am for you to catch me.
And then I wait until that moment you stand before me arms open, eyes closed with an upturned head with lips parted waiting.
So I bend close, then closer I lean forward wrap you in my arms and whisper it's you...
And then I sigh ...

The Essence Of

Tick tock, tick tock, tick tock, time the essence of.

I blink for a moment and it seems as if the hours have flown by.

So I close my eyes and ask myself what is it that I want? What is it that I feel?

And… my answer is life…

You see, I have grown from a child to a boy and now I am a man.

I have seen and experienced the dreams and illusions of my childhood, cried the tears and shed the frustration of my boyhood, and now that I am a man I live reality.

Which for me is the essence of.

Faith, honor, love…

Slowly I repeat the words again; faith, honor, love.

Faith, honor, love…

I listen to the sound of the words as they roll off my tongue and think of my life, about the things that I have done and wanted to do.

I look at all of the time I have spent dreaming of what I thought my life should be, that I've missed some of the best moments in time.

For instance breakfast at sunrise, enjoying the day just because, or learning how to relax, laugh, and live for the moment.

You see the time management, the work and striving to be the best I've mastered.

Shall we say the hard things, however, it's the small things we forget or overlook that sometimes makes the biggest difference.

Like the simple words; I love you, yes I am thinking of you and I am here for you always. Love …

If I could only get you to see what I see and feel the things I hold inside then you would know the true meaning of what my love is.

And when I say that I love you, you would understand; that for me, I am not just speaking the words.

You would understand that for me, it is my faith, my honor, and my love.

I say again that it is my faith, my honor, and my love.

It is who I am and defines the essence of…

Stolen Moments in Time

A smile, your laughter, my tears, your frown and sometimes your questions and my answers are a part of my stolen moments in time.

You see there are times when my life comes to a halt or a branching of the road and the only thing that inspires me to go on is a remembered word or your smile.

I can think of when we first met and how we sat and just talked, or I remember how I just smiled to myself thinking of how our conversation evolved.

How the words spoken took on a life of their own and wrapped and intertwined into a picture we could both see and understand.

And then I think of what you said about life and how you live for the moment and I think; stolen moments in time.
Then I smile...

All the while thinking to myself; that you are so easy to talk too and that you are so very sexy and appealing.

Then I smile a little more and you ask what, what is it that I'm smiling about and the only answer I can give is.

An even bigger smile...

As I take a moment to gather my thoughts to answer your question.
First I think of the physical attraction and how just the sight of you is pleasing to my eyes.

Or I think of how the sight of you standing makes me want to just hold you close and let you feel my desire.

Then I think of our talks the things you've said and how you say them, your wants, beliefs, and I can feel my heart burn with desire to be understood by you.

So, I answer your question by simply saying: I'm smiling because of you, I'm remembering this moment.

Slow Dance with Me

I have stood in the shadows and watched you dance.
I have stood in the shadows and watched you dance.
I stand in the shadows and watch you dance.

I am captivated by your movement and your body's grace.

I stare mesmerized by all of the random thoughts the sight of you brings.

So I move out of the shadows into the light hoping that you will catch a glimpse of me as I watch you dance.

Hoping that you will make that sexy turn and look up and see me standing, watching you dance.

So I move closer so I have a clearer view of you.

Anticipating the moment when our eyes meet and you notice me.

I am still mesmerized by your body's movement.

I am hypnotized by your body's grace and by you...

And as you dance I can see your smile of enjoyment...

See the sheen of sweat as it moisturizes your skin and hair...

I am stirred by the sight of you as you move to the rhythm of the song...

Dance... Dance... Dancing...

And I feel your vibes flowing like the beat of the music.

Thump ... Thump... Thumping ...

And I am content just watching you. Thinking ...

108

Thinking of all of the many things I would like to say but won't.

Thinking of how the sight of you dancing inspires me to ask will you slow dance with me?

Thinking of how I can approach you and start a conversation without being rejected.

Thinking, oh damn … I like how you move.

I like how you dance… The way that you dance… Your rhythm and how you are so much a part of the music.

Your flow…And how your essence flows through me captivating my every sense.

Demanding that I ask you to dance with me… Please dance with me…You have me waiting for you to slow dance with me…

Your essence is hypnotic… Your dance is erotic… And me I am still mesmerized standing in the shadows.

Remember Me

Heavenly Father we come before you asking in this prayer understanding. We ask that you grant us the strength to endure the trials we are facing and that you shelter us in your ever-loving arms.

Amen.

Dear mother walk with me.

I would like for you to smile at the memories of what my life has been.

The small trials of my childhood...

The challenges of my teen years...

And: the start of manhood...

You see when you look back upon it I want you to see that you have always been my guide.

I want you to know that you have always been the inspiration that I aspired too.

And that you are loved...

Listen... I know that at this moment the anger... The tears... And the hurt and pain is all that you feel.

And the questions of why this has happened and the answers given can't be understood.

However... I would like to say that when you think of me smile at the memories.

When you think of me remember the good times.

110

And when you think of me and you look at the possibilities of what my life could have been. Remember...

I want you to remember that my life is and has been filled with the love of my family and my friends.

I want you to remember that my life was one of happiness and joy.

That it was a life filled with laughter and smiles.

You see I can picture myself standing here beside you asking that you remember the memories we made, the tears we cried together, and the lessons you taught.

 I can stand proud before you and say that I tried to make you proud of me and that I tried to show you that your love was not in vain.

I tried... So please remember...

Now stop and look back at the picture of my life the view of what once was.

Now close your eyes and remember...

Picture in your mind an open field in the sunlight that stretches to the horizon. That's open... That's free... And that's lovely... Now picture me home...

This is, my farewell and how I want you to remember me...

My Silent Conversation

Softly
Rarely do I speak of the desires and dreams of my heart and mind.

Rarely do I speak of my silent conversations but because you have asked this once I will.

First, I want to say that to me you are my friend... My lover... And the fulfillment of the dreams I have dreamed of.

My inspiration and that I love you.

Once, I thought that to tell you the words I love you would change me or once you heard me say it that somehow it would change you.

I thought that you knew the depth of my feelings without me having to say the words.

I thought that you could feel the intensity of my feelings as I held you close.

Or that you understood that when I kiss your soft lips that I fell within your aura and that it enfolds me and makes me want to hold you tighter, kiss you deeper and fall into our world lost in time. Our magic...

Once I thought to tell you of the joy I feel as our eyes touch and the essence of you flows through me.

Of, the moment in time when I felt our heartbeats align and I whispered your name. And I cried...

Regrettably...

Once I thought to tell you, but the moment passed us by.

You see I was too busy hearing the things that you said.

More time... I heard you.

112

More communication… I opened my mind to the concepts of you.

More us … I believed in you.

I thought that I could give you the blueprint of my life so that you could read the picture and understand the plotting… The planning…

I thought that I could show you the course of my life the reasons for my action and you would understand me.

I thought that for once just once that the closeness I felt the ties that bound us was strong enough to hold us true to each other.

I thought that the ties that bound us were strong enough to weather the small disappointments, disagreements and pain.

I thought…

And then somewhere along the way you changed walked away and said no goodbyes.

Knowingly I tell you that I miss you, need you, respect you, want you, and desire you while understanding that the decision has been made and the moment has passed us by.

My Last Tear

Silence ...

I sit alone thinking of you and the times we've shared and I sigh.

I think of what I feel for you and the longing to hear your voice, feel your touch brings tears to my eyes.

So I close them tight thinking of what once was, thinking of what I thought would be and now what is.

Silence and I sigh

I close my eyes once again but, this time it's to remember and yet the only thing I can do is feel.

My thoughts stop and I feel myself yearning for you, needing you and all that you are.

Then as the teardrops slowly fall my heart seem to expand and my world shifts and I fall.

Still hoping and thinking that you love me enough to call, hoping that you love me enough to catch me.

And then I finally hit the bottom and the force of my landing tells me otherwise.

The pain of my landing tells me that I am still feeling, and for one moment I delve deep within myself and let the feelings flow.

I flood my mind with the emotions I've locked away inside and just feel.

For one heartbeat I open my heart and soul to myself and let go remembering, giving all that I am to the memory of you.

Then I close my eyes and sigh.

I shake my head thinking, feeling, and knowing that I am alone.

And again I sigh still feeling all of the love that I feel for you being drained away.

Or as the emptiness of my thoughts flow through me, I feel my tears wash away the broken dreams and the unfulfilled promises.

So I open my eyes and look at myself, I look inward and see my pain the shadows of the tears I've cried.

The shadows of the pain I hold inside.

I look inward and feel my pain and the loneliness beckons.

So I reach out to you, arms open, heart yearning and you retreat from me.

One step, then another until finally the moment arrives;

It is now decision time, so I kneel down and bow my head and cry, my last tear.

Maudlin Conversation

Once long ago it was said that to desire is to dream of and the desires of the heart: well they are heavens rewards...

For what person has not chosen his desired friend, whether they have proven their worth or merit still, there is no doubt nor fear that one's faith shall not prevail.
Once it seems a lifetime ago I heard my mom say choose your friends wisely not because of what they have or because of what they may do for you.

She said think of trust... think about character... And then think of what you are willing to give of yourself...

You see a friend is more than hi how are you, let's go party or loan me this or loan me that.

A friend or friendship is getting down in the trenches with your fresh whites on, it is saying yes when your brain is screaming no... No... No... No!

It is the disagreeing silently yet being the first to stand firm when the chips are down.

It is being ever vigilant and the walking in hand and hand... Shoulder to shoulder forever leaning on and rejoicing in the happiness of the other even through each trial and much anguish.

It is Grace ...

Heavenly Father I come before thee asking in humble prayer that on this day you bless me and those around me.

That on this day you strengthen our faith in each other and let us rejoice in another day... Another year my birthday...

That you keep us in your ever loving arms and I thank you Lord for the many blessings you have given me. My health… My family… And: my friends…

Amen

For what person has more worth than one in whom we call friend?

Love

They say that love is with the right person beautiful.
They say that love for some is quick and painless.
They say that for some love strikes at first sight.
And then they say that for most love is as illusive as the proverbial will of wisp.
It is like catching smoke during a windstorm.
Love... What exactly is it and how do I define it?
Let's see, I have read that love is the greatest feeling that one person can have for another.
I have read in the Bible of the greatest act of love, which was Gods gift of his son to save all humanity.
Now that is love on a scale so grand that it is simply awesome. It is simply inspiring...
I have read and read poetry where the poet writes about the virtue of love, the aspects of love and how love is.
They write about moon lit nights, starry skies, soft smooth skin and sexy eyes, a kiss, and an embrace. The physical...
I have heard women talk and I smile at the response they give of how love is or should be.
They speak of love with such distinction in terms of being one with their partner.
They speak of love with such fervor, with so much passion that to them love is mystical.
For some it is the spiritual binding of one to another.
The essence of knowing and sharing a bond that has no boundaries and that transcends normal rational thoughts.
In other words they are hooked... They are caught up and crazy in love.
Love... What exactly is it and what do I know about it?
Without a moment hesitation I can say I know everything to know about love.
Then again as I sit here and question myself, I will say that I know very little or nothing about love.
You see the more I think the more it is that I realize that love is more than mere words.
It is more than a physical yearning for a simple touch or a caress.
It is more than a thought of togetherness expressed by a longing or the act of just being present, the act of just going through the motions.

118

To me love is the true essence of my heart desire.
It is the purity of our thoughts, our actions, and our touch.
It is in its truest form unconditional.
And for me it is the thought I have of you when I close my eyes and cry my tears just because.
It is the lingering touch of your kiss, the feel of your body as I hold you close and smell the fragrance of you and wish with every fiber of my being that we become as one.
That: I lose myself within you or you within me.
It is the opening of my heart, the tearing down of all the walls and saying here I am, my soul is yours.
Love me…

A Glimpse of Tomorrow

Yesterday… I awoke and dreamed of how my day would be.

I envisioned that for once the sun would shine bright and that things would happen for me.

Good things…

Like getting the call for lunch and dinner from that special someone or flowers just because.

Or maybe it would be just a phone call to say hi I was thinking of you and decided to call.

No bells, no whistles, or alarms just a call.

It would be my day to enjoy with a smile, the small simple things, yes the good things.

However, that was yesterday and today… well

I awoke and looked at how yesterday was, and I am hoping that today will not be the same.

You see that special someone that I spoke of before didn't call.

And those flowers that were supposed to be just because never arrived.

And oh! Were there bells, whistles and alarms?

I swore and cried, laughed once and cried some more and then!

I met you and you took a moment of your time to ask was I okay?

Was there anything that you could do to help?

And from that moment on yesterday didn't matter and my today well let's say that it is beginning to be the yesterday I dreamed of.

120

Because, as we talked the tears dried up I laughed more and smiled.

Those feelings of being alone, weak and discouraged I put aside and it was then that I saw my glimpse of tomorrow.

Dreaming... Smiling... Laughing... Loving... And being loved...

It was then that I realized that the yesterdays bring us too and show us our today and the today's are the shadows of our yesterdays that reflect upon the glimpse of our tomorrows.

Yesterday... Today... and a glimpse of tomorrow...

Yesterday… today… and a glimpse of tomorrow…

A Good Man

A woman's man he is infectious... Sensual... Strong... Determined... Respectful... fallible and yet infallible... He is human.

He is a man of his word inspiring those around him.

He is a man of distinction demanding respect and giving it in return.

He is a man of his word upholding the values that he hold dear. His gentleman's code...

You know ladies those not so secret desires that you wished all men had or should have.

Honor... Respect... Trust... Love... Commitment... and Communication...

A gentleman and a charmer he is perceptive and a romantic who think of candle lit nights filled with roses and rose petals.

While listening to soft romantic music and slow dancing to your favorite songs.

He holds you close tempted by the sway of your body with his, tempted and willing to anticipate and explore your woman's need.

So listen as I share with you this tempting picture of a good man, a sensitive man, and a caring man.

Now open your eyes and mind to the concept of a man who is in touch with his emotions and who is unafraid to share them, who is unafraid to share his tears... his disappointment... and his fears...

He is a listener with the patience to know when to speak and has the sensitivity to know when the moment is right to act.

He is a good man.

A man who is always thinking of more ways of becoming better...

A man who is always thinking of more ways to make you smile...

A man who is always thinking of ways to show you that he will be there always to make things better to show you that you are a special lady...

And that he is a man that will be there to try and make things right to make them better always.

That you are to him his sunshine and the real reason that he strives to let you know that chivalry like him is still to be found.

Impossible, non-existent you say this man is but a figment of words and song.

Then I say open your mind to the concept of visualizing this man and to the concept of romance and then just believe.

I say open your heart to the concept that he is your shining knight, the sunshine within your shadows and your shelter from life storms.

And to him your smile is his sunshine the reason he strives to be a good man, your good man.

He is a scholar... A gentleman... A dreamer and mind reader... He is yours...

A Pause in Time

Once long ago it seemed as if my life was destined.

It seemed as if the sun shone on my rainy days, and the storm clouds built but only provided shade for me on those hot, hot days.

And the world was spinning to a rhythm that I knew, that I could feel and that I could relate too.

Or so I thought... For behold, times changed and the world, kept on spinning...

And I watched as we grew individually as a people and then as a nation.

I watched as the fall of pride, prejudices, ignorance and hatred went from being open and forthright to being hidden in soft words and sweet smiles.

I watched as that friendly handshake and pat on the back fell from grace and became an illusion. Wasted motion...

I watched and the world kept on spinning.

Once long ago they said that an education would make a difference.

They implied that with an education times would change and it would give me equality and enhance my freedom.

They said that an education could and would help me achieve the American dream.

That it would give me stature and a position that I could be proud of.

They said that with an education I could stand and be heard no longer subjected to being stigmatized as inferior, illiterate and uneducated.

And I say they lied…

Maybe, just maybe for that select, select few… For that less than one percent an education can and does make a difference. Maybe…

However: when you look at me and without a question or a doubt and say that I am less than you.

Or when, you see the face that I wear and say to yourself that I am ignorant and dumb without listening to a word that I speak or hear the context of my conversation.

Or you look at the color of my skin and step away, closing your mind to the idea that I am a man or a woman who thinks, feel and dream the same as you.

I must ask does it really matter.

And then you wonder, why for me, this moment is but a pause in time. You wonder… Why…

Once, long ago it was simply the way of the world and the way things were done for you to say and think the way you did.

However, times have changed and the world keeps on spinning…

And it is no longer a time to wonder why. It is a time to think…

It is no longer a time to wonder why. But: a time to feel…

It is no longer a time to wonder why. But: a time to listen…To consider…

A time to open your mind…

A time to be silent…

It is not, a time for you to judge me?

A Sense of You

Warning... warning... warning... still waters runs deep.

And as the saying goes, if you toss a pebble upon a still pond the ripples spread in an ever-widening pattern, sometimes not so easy to discern.

Therefore, when I think of you the saying still waters run deep fills my mind.

And! I want to lean over you and look at my reflection.

I want to look deep within your well, past the barriers, beyond the swirling, whirling cyclone that you are to the calm center. You...

Then place the tip of my finger upon your surface and watch the ripples expand.

Wondering, where will the ripples end and how deep is the well from which they began?

So I lean over your well and look at my reflection, because you intrigue me.

You have me thinking about the stillness of your water and asking myself what's beneath the surface.

You see I can sense the raging currents beneath the calm, and feel the ripples of your hidden barriers as I lean over your well and place my fingertip within your essence.

And oh! Such power as this I now realize the full meaning for the no trespassing.

So I remove my fingertip and lean over your well again and look at my reflection.

Only this time I think of your well spilling over a waterfall tumbling, rumbling, drop after drop breaking through all barriers.

A force of uncontainable power, you know that calm center. Your stillness.

Or I think of hurling myself into your well so I can become the reflection you see as you lean over my well to see your reflection.

And I see the ripples expand ring by ring and I wonder where will they end.

How will they touch you and what will be the response?

Slowly as each ring reverberates to the essence of your touch I become aware of your true persona.

I become aware of your faith, your love, and your desires.

I become aware of the thoughts you have, your worries and your fears.

I become aware of your dreams, your nightmares, the good and the bad.

I become aware of all things but mostly a sense of you.

And as the ripples expand and I see my reflection, touch your essence and breathe at that moment it is you.

It is everything and I am simply a reflection of the image from the reflection of you.

Beyond That Great Goodnight

Beyond that great goodnight I wonder, I think about the stages of my life and I ponder.

I ask myself questions and think about the answers I give and then I ask myself the question.

Which is am I satisfied with my life, can I do better than I am doing, what is it that I want of life or is this what I have all that I expect?

And then I have a revelation simple yet true and that is, that life is beyond a doubt simply amazing.

It holds for each of us so many possibilities that our perception of it is flawed.

Think on that and then ask yourself how... And why...

Now listen as I explain.

I close my eyes and let the images flow from my brain to my soul to my minds eye.

You see they say that the eyes are the windows to our soul therefore, they show each thought and every emotion.

The tears we have cried, sections of the roads we have walked, our timeless memories, our timeless wonders, the stolen moments in time, our dreams, and our future and all the moments in between.

Shhh! Now listen as I express to you the vision of this world hope in the faces of our children.

I read their destiny from their laughter and their smiles.

I see the wisdom gained from the compassion shown, the decisions made and from the trials they face.

I see the disappointment in the tears they cry and have cried and yet that ray of hope still shines.

And from that beacon springs a dedicated commitment and they rise into maturity after being knocked down. Down... Down... And down...

They rise... You see maturity isn't defined by a number but is defined by how a person accepts the roles that life demand they live.

It is defined by the number of times we rise up from being knocked down and wiping ourselves off and trying again.

It is the learning from life's mistakes and taking that extra moment while down to plan the next move, a moment to take a moment if you will.

And yes... It is that moment when it seems as if they are standing upon the edge of the world balanced staring from horizon to horizon trying to find their guiding light

And... It is at that moment in time when the world spins and their destiny is revealed.

And it is not the fame and glamour they dreamed of, nor is it the wealth of millions, neither diamonds nor gold.

It is not the fancy homes, the expensive cars or fancy clothes. But, much more...

It is... A lifetime of memories... A stolen moment in time... A viewed sunrise...

A sunset or moonrise...That first moment of falling in love... Your first kiss...

That moment in time when you realize that your wealth... Your destiny is your family, your friends, and your memories...

129

And your legacy is your great goodnight…

Contained and Released

I pause and consider the words you have spoken.
And I understand I think, what you have said.

However, when I really look at our time together, the hours, the minutes, it's like a magician show that is mostly hot air and disappearing smoke.

You see the promises made I believed you would keep.

And when you said you loved me, well, I believed.

I thought at last that there was someone in my life who would be there from that moment on.

I thought that for once, there was no more being alone.

Because I had you to talk with, I could share that part of me I always kept locked away.

The fears... my doubts...

That part of me that being with you somehow found a release.

In other words my feelings were no longer contained.

And... then... you changed and like the magician's smoke you disappeared.

And with no reason nor an explanation all I do is sit, think, and relive the times we shared.

I go over the memories one by one at times in slow motion.

Or I pause over a remembered word or phrase; thinking, thinking, thinking.

And then I'm jolted from my trance and realize that I'm just staring into space, so I smile, shake my head and close my eyes.

You see by reliving the memories, I'm learning and seeing some of the things I've missed.

I have finally understood that for you, our time the moments we shared was just that a moment and it has passed.

Just as your words of love, the caring, the talks, the sharing are all gone.

So, have I been released.

Generations

I look back over the years I have lived and see the different stages of change in my life and I am amazed.

You see we started out in our homeland as kings and queens a united people filled with our pride and strength.

Conquerors, statesmen, rulers, builders, inventors, teachers, and physicals beyond compare.

Our history is rich and colorful, known but not taught.

It has been set aside to be viewed at random.

Our legacy spoken in three words, defined as blood... sweat... tears...

Our blood, our sweat, and our tears for some it is a living testimony of an era they lived.

The past... the present... the future...

Our past remembered in anger, filled with the horror of deeds best left cloaked in darkness and shadows.

It was a time when the morality of a nation and its people was tested and found wanting.

It was a time when the greed and status of the minority, was more important than the greater good.

It was a time when our blood ran red due to the midnight beatings, the late night hangings or shooting.

It was a time when the blood ran cold at the thought of our sons and daughters missing.

It was time when our blood ran cold at the thought of our loved ones being found alongside a lonely country road dead.

133

It was our reality and our blood that was shed and it was our past...

Our past... It is a past that we remember because we live it...

I know because we lived through it...

I know because I can still feel the sweat and tears from our bodies as we sweltered in the heat upon the decks and within the holds of the slave ships that brought us here?

I know because I can feel the sweat and tears from our bodies as we worked the plantations as cheap dispensable slave laborers?

I can feel the sweat and the tears from our bodies knowing that we were bound and chained in slavery, with the slimmest hope hidden deep within us of one day being free? Escaping...

I can feel the hope, yet, know despair knowing that to be free meant you would be leaving your loved ones behind. Your strength...

Can you feel me? Can you understand the anguish we have felt, can you hear our souls crying or see the fields soak in our blood?

We have adapted and adjusted, we have cried and mourned, been silent and screamed to the world that we want freedom and that we deserve better.

We have said that we are here and yes, this is a part of our past... It is our strength and our weakness... Our blood... Our sweat... And: our tears...

Remember...

I was once told that in life you have to know where you come from in order to know where you are going.
In other words your heritage... Your past... The present... Your future...

Your heritage is the foundation from which you build and your past is the reference from which you learn.

Whereas: the present is the here and now and how you choose to live and your future why that is the legacy you give.

You see we came from a nation strong in our strength, our pride, our beliefs and traditions.

We built civilizations from our sweat, our blood, and our tears that lasted hundreds of years.

Had great kings and queens that ruled empires with such skill that their influence is still felt to this day.

Such as: King Akhenaton the creator of monotheism and his wife, Queen Nefertiti.

Hannibal, the ruler of Carthage and who is considered one of the greatest general and military strategist who ever lived.

Imhotep: the father of medicine, an architect, astronomer, philosopher, poet, and the first recorded multi genius.

Shaka Zulu: warrior, leader and civilization builder.

Queen Makeda the symbol of beauty.

Queen Nandi the mother of Shaka Zulu and known as the symbol of a woman of high esteem.

And Yaa Asantewa warrior queen.

Remember... this is a part of our past...

Remember... this is our legacy, the well from which we draw our strength, our pride.

Remember... this is the well from which our heritage flows.

Remember... once we were a nation of great kings, great queens, scholars, architects, statesmen's, rulers, inventors, teachers, and physicians beyond compare.

Remember... because this is our past... our present... our future...

Remember... Generations...

I Am a Mother's Child

This is for the one woman in my life who has given me the most. Who has taught me the most.

And who still give, teach, and loves me with an unconditional love that breaches all boundaries.

I am talking about my mother... You see time and time again I sit and think of my life, the once upon a time not so long ago.

Compare it to the life I live now and that I am surrounded by.

And: I must say that I am glad that I am a mother's child.

You see I look at the tragedies we see and hear of daily.

I listen to the different discussions about values, the lack of morals, and the human capacity to feel for others and ourselves.
Then I sit some more and think...

Years ago, it was A blight upon society, when the crimes were committed by the unsavory characters of the underworld. The mob or mobsters... Drug lords or drug deals gone bad...Or the habitual criminal...
Years ago... And: now?

We see the faces of the unsavory character staring at us face to face from our children's eyes.

We see the unsavory character watching us from across the street from our neighbor's windows... their fence line...

From the television we watch... the music we hear... The games we play... Violence...

In fact it is the very essence of our life.

I once read that there is a thin veneer that separates barbarism from being civilized.

I once read that the difference that made man master of his destiny and other animals is his capacity to think and reason.

Civilized man master of his destiny. Ruler...

Civilized man, reverting... reverting... reverting... Civilized man trapped within the chaos of his own mind. A Destroyer...

And then I read about the tragedy at Columbine High School... The Amish Schoolhouse...And now Virginia Tech University...

And now I wonder what has happen to; our civilized Society...
I wonder... I wonder... I wonder...And then.

I ponder upon the question where is the empathy?

I ponder upon the question where is the compassion?

I ponder upon the question where is civilized man embittered cry that enough is enough?

Where is civilized man embittered cry that we are losing our children and the violence has to stop?

Where is it?

I take a moment to sit and listen and the only cry that I hear is the weeping voice of a mother asking what did I do wrong?

The only voice I hear is a mother crying my child is gone...

The only Cry that I hear is a mother mourning a mother's child.

And I wonder: where is our civilized society?

The empathy, the compassion, civilized man master of his destiny. Ruler...

Civilized man... A mother's child...

138

I Hear Your Whispers

Three strings three bars and a melody of sound that transcends the boundaries of the physical mind.

As I lay down to sleep it filters through the low hum of background noise and I hear. Your whispers...

You see it has been ten days nine hours forty-five minutes and thirteen seconds.

Ten days... Nine hours... Forty-five minutes... And thirteen seconds... Which is: to too long...

I could do the thirteen seconds forty-five minutes the nine hours and maybe even stretch it to one or two days.

I could improvise and deceive myself into thinking that time is not just dragging by.

Or I could throw myself into the activities of the day and try to forget but for ten days. That is to too long...

Listen I have an imagination that can take me from here to some fantasies that would blow your mind.

I have an imagination that can travel from here to the stars, to the moon and back again without missing a beat or to pause.

However, when I think of you it does.

It's like the world pauses and you float in on a melody of sound so pure that the only thing I hear is, your whisper.

And the only thing I feel is the beat of my heart bump, bump, bumping to the melodious whispers that call to me.

Once long, long ago it seems...

Eight years twenty-one days nine hours forty-seven minutes and fifty-one seconds I heard your whispers and followed my dream.

And now eight years twenty-one days nine hours forty-seven minutes and fifty-one seconds later I still hear your whispers and I am here asking do you love me?

I am here asking when I am alone in the night and the world ceases to spin and topples into oblivion will I hear you? Your whispers...

Again I am asking when I am alone in the night and the stars have ceased to inspire a poets words of inspiration will you come to me?

Or will I only hear the fading echo of your whisper as I drift off to sleep and dream of...

The yesterdays gone... My tomorrows to come... And the whispers you speak...

Listen, I can hear your whispers... And I am asking am I yours... Are you mine?

Do you love me?

Another Day

Another day, a sunrise meant for us to savor together, yet I experience it alone with my thoughts, my memories, my love, my pain, and my tears

One by one they fall as I ache for you, your voice, your smile, your scent, your touch, your heart beating in rhythm with mine, I thought it was forever

Another day, I think of you and wonder where you are, how you are and do I ever cross your mind? I try to move on, let it go, trust that God has a plan

Days pass, I still wonder, I find myself reliving scenes of our time, like a favorite old black and white movie, a classic etched permanently in my mind, my heart, my body and soul

Another day, a sunset takes my breath away as pieces of my heart slip away, are you there? Are you thinking of me too? I feel you but it fades as the sunset disappears and darkness settles in, you are no where to be found

It all seems so easy for you, to walk away without a fight, no regret, no wonder of what could have been, no tears for a smile that made my day, for the voice that was a song unheard by any other, for the touch that was the love I dreamed of, that pure joy of being with another so completely

Another day comes and goes, weeks pass, now months and I cry again, exploding with the feelings that were not returned, of the love that was not welcomed, God help me let it go, I am falling, lost in a mist of tears and memories

Night falls, sleep is not easy, and the clock ticks in beat with my own heart, my pillow dampened by the tears I fight. Finally, sleep comes and I dream of my love being and how wonderful it must be, I awake and it is a dream

141

Another day, I have now lost hope, though my love remains in tact; I pray for peace and try to move on, as I know God would have me

do. Again tears fall, guilt beckons at my door, my heart locked and sealed, another treats me like a Queen, yet I am not free, my heart and soul belong to another.

Today, I saw you, I try to keep it together but I fall again, lost in the memories of us, of the man I still love, of the man I dream of, of the man who was my sunshine on the rainiest of days, of the man I wished loved me like I love him

Today, I prayed for you, that you are well, happy; that life is treating you well. I wonder if you have found the love I speak of and then, I am torn between happiness for you and a deep sadness that I wasn't the one.

Another day, I smile because although my love was not returned I feel love and know that it was real, completely without resolve, I gave myself to you and did the best I could. .

Today, I am a better woman because of you, I imagine love more deeply, I have grown, I will be more patient, I will be more understanding, I will be more prepared for the love God has for me and I will fight for it, I will not let it go for I know that love just is and there is no guarantee for another day!

This day the tears come unbidden and the memories flash across my mind like a stream of images in a slideshow.

I see the distant scenes of us together hear the sound of your laughter and can envision the sight of my face with a simple smile.

You see even though I didn't laugh out loud, even though I didn't try and become the main attraction I always enjoyed our times together, for me the explosions were inside.

142

I just didn't know how to express them so that you could see them.

I just didn't know how to tell you that when you where around the sun shone even on my rainy days.

I didn't know how to show you that you meant more to me than just a second or a third thought throughout the day.

I didn't know and even when you spoke I heard every word.

However to me I wanted to give you the things that I believed you deserved I wanted to give you the things that was in my heart.

I wanted to take you places and show you all of the things that no one else ever had, I wanted to be worthy of the love you was giving.

My fears are and were that you didn't understand.

Terry Cole

Our Story

Sometime, in nightmares I remember...

I remember as a child the grandeur in which we lived. The prestige... The home... And the land from which we came...

I remember the sense of stability and security that all of those things combined with the love of my parents did give.

Until that faithless day our world changed. War...

The day our world of stability became fragile and filled with uncertainty.

The day that my security became a day of fleeing never certain of what the next moment would bring.

It was the day I realized that there would never be anything certain except the fact that unless we kept on moving death was a surety.

Sometime, when I awake from my nightmares I remember.

I remember crying and telling my parents that I want to go home. I want to go home...

Not understanding that to return home would mean certain death.

Not understanding that to survive, my young life would change even more and that I would see and experience things that would take me to the edge of an abyss that a lifetime of living couldn't bring me back from.

That a lifetime of mourning couldn't heal me from...

I remember... I remember as we were packed nineteen people to a twenty-one foot boat and set out to sea. Refugees...

144

And I remember the total sense of hopelessness as wave after wave pounded our small world.

I remember the feel of the water upon my face as we floated day by day filled with the fears of the unknown.

I remember each moment wondering if we would survive to the next.

I remember sometimes in my nightmares the feel of the water as it flows from the punctured hole in our boat, and then wondering what's next. And then just waiting...

I remember watching as my uncle dove overboard willing to sacrifice himself trying to repair the leak in order that everyone else could survive. Our family...

And I remember our collective sigh of relief, as he emerged from the water for the final time cold yet safe.

And I remember the tears I cried as I saw the ship that would rescue us and change our lives, that would transport us from a world filled with dread and fear to one of hope and unlimited possibilities.

I remember... Sometimes in my nightmares I remember.

I remember and sometimes I think back and thank God that we survived.

I remember... I am a refugee and this is our story.

A Time to Fly

I think of you as my baby.

Remember how small and vulnerable you were so tiny, so innocent, and so sweet.

Your tiny hands and feet I can still feel.

The sound of your cry when you were hungry I still hear.

Your smile I still see in my mind's eye and I can still feel the imprint of your body as I held you.

Let's just say the captured memories.

Now looking back down through the years I see the pictures of you growing first as an infant, then as a toddler and now as a young adult.

I stand upon the sidelines and watch as you rise from the shadows like the sun shining through the morning mist.

I watch as the image of who you are shines brighter and brighter as you grow into the person you are.

I watch and see the world tip upon its axis and I am amazed.

That not only am I seeing and living this evolution of change in you but the world also.

I am amazed that as you rise and the world around you is full of chaos and panic you remain humble and simple.

I am amazed that as your peers and confidants jockey for the riches, the fame, and glamour that you simply take it all in stride.

And me I laugh, I smile, I take it all in of who you are and then I ask myself how did you learn to fly so well?

146

A Touch of Class

I have seen you grow from an infant to a young lady.

I have experienced your smile, and your charm.

And now I believe that I'm beginning to see you come into your own your style.

Your smile is bigger, with a great deal more flare.

Your tone is firmer with that authoritative snap.

And your stance, well, let's just say that you got the walk, the pride and the style.

I remember not long ago when you were shy, soft spoken, timid and sweet.

And now?

Well I will say that the proof is in the pudding, and as the song goes look at you now.

Bold as the sun in all of its glory.

You are just as bright as the sun when it shines upon the world.

And like the sun your smile, your aura shines so very bright.

While the spirit within you beginning to awaken like a tender flower.

And like the suns light I your father am beginning to see you blossom and become the exotic flower you are.

A Moment Away

From the shadows rising comes forth a young man of Promise.
He is a parent's hope of dreams fulfilled.
He is their legacy.

Imbued with the spirit of generations past he is one moment away
from the distant shores of Panama and his heritage.

He is one moment away from home.

Of the stories told about what once was he has heard a few.

Of the pictures taken and the scenes remembered they are his.

And of a mother's joy's her sorrows and expectations they are
mine.

I have watched you grow from a bump into this falling down child
to one of grace and form.

From that shy always want to be around me child to one bold and
willful.

From, being my baby to being a young man.

From the mist and shadows a picture emerges of a young man
strong in character, tempered in love and still a dreamer.

A dreamer who still believes that life has equality without pain…

A dreamer who still thinks that money grows on trees and who
believes that talent and not luck and a great deal of hard work will
ensure success.

A dreamer who believes that life is a page yet to be written.

Historically I will journey back to a time and place where an
education was a parents dream unlike now when the dream is of
fame and fortune.

I will journey back to a time where it was believed that our future, our hope was and is our children the next generation.

Where, the dream of each parent was to see their child rise from the birth of infancy, to their teen years and from there to an acceptance of adulthood.

Where, it was a parent's dream to sit and think of the moments yet to come, high school graduation, college graduation, a good job and possibly someday marriage and maybe grandchildren.

Where, it was a parent's dream just to dream.

And today we smile, we laugh and we will cry because; today it is no longer a parent's dream. But reality...

And I want you to know that you are my labor of love and I am a moment away.

Forever

It's odd that I a person who have always said that all things have a beginning and an end should now want forever.

It's odd that no matter how many times that I have said no in the past that I should fall within the trap called love and forget that there is no forever.

And it is all because of you... And now I am lost...
In terms of distance it would seem as if I have traveled the world over, mile for mile.

It would seem as if each mile has turned into a reflection of the love we share, the talks we had and our moments.

Forever...

It's odd that I a person who believes in love should think that love is not endless.

Or, that I should open myself to its possibilities and wish that it would carry me to heights and lows that are un-herald and unparalleled.

Or, that I could just accept this feeling that I have that love simply is.

Or, so it would seem...

Forever...

It's odd that I being the man that I am can look inside myself and feel the emotions inside and wish with all my being that you could at least once understand me.

That for one moment in time you could read my soul and feel the intensity and depth of what I truly am.

That for one brief instant in time my true essence touched yours.

I wish…

So I close my eyes and see the images of you and I imprinted upon my soul and I yield to the emotions calling out to me and I surrender my soul up to God in heaven.

And, I surrender my soul to God in heaven for forever.

It's odd that I a man of the world should think that true love has no ending and that no matter how many times true love captures the imagination and the human heart it is still elusive.

It is still thrilling and that it is without a doubt enchanting, intoxicating and romantic.

It is eternal but not forever.

A Generation of One

It started this journey of ours 124 years ago. The Martin and Breary legacy...
Of our family... Of our heritage... Of our honor and our pride.
It is thirteen generations of the memories of our family, of our walk through time and of the things that once was, is and shall be. Our family's dreams... The values... Our rules...
Thirteen generations of joy, of sharing, and of belonging.
Our heritage... Our Family... Our honor and our pride...
Behold we stand under the hands of time and pay homage to our elders.
We gather in song and dance and remember the hugging, the kissing, and the goodbyes.
We come together as a family connecting and interweaving our lives strand-by-strand and building upon the legacy.
Of our heritage... Our family... Our honor and our pride...
I look around me and see the diversity and I smile.
I see our elders sitting quietly, regal, for they are our crown jewels.
They are irreplaceable... They are wisdom and knowledge... They are patience and understanding, love, commitment and teachers.
I see our elders and I realize that they are our foundation, our future, our past and our shield.
They are solid ground from which to build. Our foundation...
They are the rules, the values and the dreams we live for. Our future...
They are the morning dawn on the hardships faced. Our past.
They are the lessons learned. Our shields...
I see our elders and I think of the Martin and Breary union so long ago and I think of the sacrifices made.
I think of the hardships that we have endured and I kneel before my God in heaven and just say a silent prayer of thanks.
I thank him for the ability to stand before you and acknowledge that we are a family in whom the word family has gotten stronger from generation to generation.
I thank him for the elders who sit among us now and for those who have journeyed on. For the scholars in waiting: their cloak, their mantle soon they will put on.
And for the children for you see the legacy must go on.
And I thank Him... And I thank Him... And I thank Him...

152

And then I ask him to forgive me and for the strength to forgive others.

I ask him to cleanse my heart and to heal my tender wounds.

I asked Him in prayer that we draw closer together mother to daughter, son to father, sister-to-sister, brother-to-brother and family-to-family.

For we are Love... We are Forgiveness... And we are Family...

I asked...

It started this journey of ours 124 years ago and thirteen generations later.

I stand before you asking that we remember the greatness of love.

That we remember the fullness of love...

And that we are the recipients of both one family A Generation Of One...

The Martin/Breary Family...

In Myths and Legends

To be or not to be this is my question.
They say that in life there is a thin line between love and hate.

They say that in life true love is the ultimate experience that a person can feel.

They say that it is majestic… That it is subjective… And, that it is divine.

In myths and legends…

In reality I stand-alone, in a world of myths and legends and they are only myths and legends.

I can close my eyes and sense the emptiness of the void around me, I can feel the desolation of the void inside me and I think of myths and legends.

In myths and legends there is always the dashing knight in his bright Armor to rescue the princess in distress.

There's always the dashing hero to save the day but in reality like now there is only the desolate tears of sorrow and despair.

There is only the unfulfilled longing inside of wanting to be a part of something that is greater than who or what you are.

There is only the unshed tears you cry to try and wash away the dread you feel when you close your eyes and picture your life.

In myths and legends this would be the time when that hero would appear and make things right.

In myths and legends…

But in reality this is the one moment in time when the world shifts the sky falls and you tumble into a darkness soul deep.

154

It is that point in time when life is balanced upon a dreams edge and you dare not wake.

That moment in time when all of life dreams the promises your tomorrows the yesterdays in the blink of an eye disappear.

It is that moment in time when our doubts become reality.

It is that moment in time when we look at the two alternatives. Life... Death...

They say that in life there are two absolutes life, death, and one thing more the fillers in between.

Breathing... Seeing... Feeling... Loving... Living... Experiencing... Falling and Rising...

I have stood outside your door a thousand times in my mind and watched you.

Or I have heard your voice it seems for several lifetimes and will continue to hear it until time is no more.

True love, in myths and legends transcends human conception it is God.

And God like...

I Imagine

I was once told that chocolate is the world most favorite candy.

And among the many flavors there are three that are the most popular. White chocolate... Mocha chocolate... and Dark chocolate...

All a blend of different flavors rich, smooth so moist and all are delicious and so, so tempting.

For me you are the Mocha chocolate a mixture of white and dark yet light and creamy the ultimate in sexy.

Hmm... Now let me taste you.

Close your eyes and picture this like the candy wrapped in its wrapper I need to unwrap you.

So first I start slow and unbutton your blouse button by button.

Until it just hangs there open to my touch and then I lean in close and inhale your fragrance.

I inhale your fragrance, I taste your fragrance, and I moan and step back and look at you my mocha surprise.

Smile, take a step closer slide your blouse over your shoulders down each arm and watch as it fall to the floor as I slowly let my eyes caress your body intimately.

I gently oh so gently do I softly pull you closer as I unbutton Ms. Gloria Secret to reveal more.

And as before I take a step back, look at you then quickly I lean forward and taste your sweetness and oh! I taste you, taste you, and taste you.

And as I slowly swirl and caress you with my tongue I listen to the quick inhale of your breath and feel your heartbeat quicken.

So I step back look again and this time I see a light film of moisture on your body, so I lean in and take you.

I lean in and slide my hands down your body down to the button on your pants and pause.

I pause and pause thinking, thinking damn! I want to taste all of you.

Thinking, thinking oh! Damn as my hand tremble as my hand slip so I pause again and look and this time I see and feel a heavy film of moisture on my body my hands.

I am hot so I take a breath hold it and exhale slowly, close my eyes and concentrate as my fingers fumble at your button.

I concentrate and then the button is undone and my hand slides over your smooth skin and I hmm.

I gently lift you and slide your pants off inch by inch, leg by leg until there is only one small piece of the wrapper left.

So I bend down for a moment and let my hand slide down your body slowly touching, touching, touching until it stop and at that moment I hear your quick indrawn breath and feel your wetness and I moan. Hmm…

I can feel myself rising, feel the palms of my hands sweating feel my desire to explore you burning hotter and hotter, I can feel my desire.

So I reach up and remove the last of the wrapping I lean over and kiss your forehead, your lips, your neck, your breast, your stomach arms and fingertips.

Then I slide down to your navel, your thighs and then I move just a little and as I slide inside you I whisper mocha, mocha, mocha I am your chocolate surprise.

I whisper it is just as I imagined it and then I release my imagination.

Forever Always

This is a tribute to the goodness of God.

This is dedicated to the greatness of God... His love, his mercy, his strength, his wisdom, his understanding and love...

Heavenly Father we come before thee this day in prayer and thanksgiving. We kneel under thine heavenly kingdom with our hearts and mind looking up to thee asking for forgiveness, asking for mercy, understanding, wisdom, knowledge, strength, and thine grace. We pray to thee humbling our hearts and mind asking for thine guidance, asking for thine help, asking Father that you help us to be worthy of thine love, of thine patience of thine grace and mercy.

Behold I stood upon the pinnacle of the world reviewing my life.

I saw the creation of the world in seven days.

The birth of Adam and Eve from a thought saw the Garden of Eden and I rejoiced.

I rode the winds of time and saw the world change and then time slowed and I saw the destruction and the salvation of the world as Noah's Ark rose upon the floodwaters of the forty days and nights of rain.

I saw the fall of Sodom and Gomorrah and I wept.

I heard God's promise to Abraham our legacy so I bowed my head in prayer calling out to him in heaven and he answered me.

He closed my eyes, and carried me to heaven's gate and showed me Abraham's legacy.

He showed me a panoramic view in detail of life and his love.

The trials we face our joys, and our tears.

He spoke to me about the choices we make their consequences sin and death.

And then he spoke of his love and within a blink of an eyelash his love washed over me, through me, and all around me it was everywhere.

And then he said: I am only a moment away when you need me close your eyes and feel me.

Close your eyes and picture me.

Close your eyes and hear me and I will open my arms and feel you one heartbeat at a time.

I will be with you forever always listening to you, always protecting you, always blessing you and loving you.

For behold I am the way the truth and the life. I am Alpha and Omega the first and the last.

For I am God, and there is none else.

My Hour of Grace

Seven days...

I awake from dreams of hardships and problems to a sunlight room of no worries.

Still, until I am fully awake the dreams persist and I remember.

Slowly as the peace of the morning and the silence enfolds me deeper within its essence the dreams fade and time flows through me.

At that moment I am time, I can sense the flow of the atoms around me, through me.

I can sense each rotation in the loop of time, count each strand of light and hear my God clearer.

And then I breathe, the moment pass and the sun still shine only not so bright and I arise giving thanks for the many blessings I have received.

I give thanks for this moment as I reflect upon life and what is.

I give thanks for the tears I have cried, the mountains I have climbed and the valleys I've crossed.

You see in grace have I been kept and the tears I've cried have washed me clean.

The mountains I have climbed have shown me the heights in life that I can achieve.

And... For the valley's I've crossed they have shown me the beauty in life, the small miracles that most overlook and never see.

And they have shown me that life is a journey filled with many wonders that can be seen if we open our eyes and believe.

161

For within the essence of my soul there are no boundaries my faith is my foundation, and grace is my life.

Behold I stare upon the reflections of the images of my family and I see the gentle flow of time passage.

I relive each definitive moment in my life my birth, my first cry, the first touch or caress of my mother and father, the first time I felt God's love.

Or I think about my family and understand that they are my hour of grace.

You see no matter what I am or what I become they have always loved me.

No matter how many times I have fallen or how many mistakes I have made they have always supported and believed in me.

They are my family, they are grace and I love them always.

Today I awake from dreams of life's hardships and sorrows.

I stroll through the avenue of my mind, look through the windows and see the boy that I was, the man that I am, and the man I shall become.

I see grace my moment, my hour, my time, it is who I am and like God's grace from heaven it is special.

My hour of grace...

It is...

The Window of My Soul

I once stood within the shadow of times flight and contemplated the actions of my thoughts and then I saw her.
A lady of beauty has wit, is a romantic, smart and energetic, strong, courageous and who is a soldier for her man.

She is a queen... She is sensual... And she is the window of my soul...

I feel her presence, her thoughts her pain and her joy.

I see her.

She is my innocence and my laughter she is a sweet quiet spirit that is unstirred by the world around her. My salvation...

My essence... Deception... For she is fragile not frail, she is strength she is strong and beautiful within.

And sometimes I wonder where does she come from? Where does she hide? How can she have such a beautiful aura untouched by the world how can she have such innocence?

And then I close my eyes and say a prayer of thanks.

And then we talked.

I conversed with her I laughed I smiled and felt as if I had known her for a lifetime.

And then she touched me and I felt something come over me.

I felt comforted and safe and I feel understood I admire her for she speaks many languages best of all she speaks mine.

I can hear her words echo through the valleys of my soul feel the passage of each as it touches my essence.

I feel...

163

I close my eyes and wonder is she real or a figment of my imagination I don't know but I want to enjoy the moments we share the memories.

I want her and again I wonder does she want me? Does she want to see me again? Or am I just another moment in time that is passing?

Slowly as time unwinds and my imagination free me from the images of my mind my soul expands and I am part of her universe.

I am the undying spark that set Rome to burning; I am the rain to a drought filled land bringing salvation and hope.

I am the pinnacle upon which the earth rotates the wheel that forever spins and which time is measured by.

I am her and she is me and together we are the windows of my soul.

Together we are one.

One heart… One word… One song… We are life…

You Touched Me

I rise to dreams of grandeur and respect.

Kneel before the altar of my God in prayer.

Sit before the mirror of destiny, stare into the world's eye and remember how you have touched me.

How you have spoken to me.

How you have counseled me.

I was once told that life is like passing through the eye of a needle.

They said that when trying to pass through it beware for it is a tight squeeze, you can see the daylight through the needles eye but getting through is a battle to achieve.

I was told…

And then, I met you and from that moment on you have touched me.

From that moment on my life was changed.

From that moment on although I never told you, you have inspired me.

You have strengthened me…

You have taught me that life joys are to be cherished and enjoyed.

You have shown me that patience, understanding, and love is a must and that family is a burden and an honor.

You have given me some precious memories.

Sometimes in my moments of clarity I see your smile and hear your voice.

I have heard the moments in time pass us by and still the moments with you are endless.

Or I remember our talks of days gone and still it is as if time has reversed itself and you are beside me.

Still talking... Still teaching... And still being the fun person you are...

My friend and mother...

My confidant and undisputed partner in mischief... The instigator...

You are loved.

Sometimes as time passes me by I relive the moments and wonder do you know how I feel for you?

Do you know what I feel for you?
Sometimes I relive the moments and smile.

I relive the moments seen through the needles eye and remember just how much you have touched me.

I see the sparkle within your eyes and know that you are a prankster.

I hear the tone of your voice and tell by its sound that mischief is growing within you and that it is about to become a full bloom.

Or I step into a room and feel your presence and I know that you are always only a moment away that you are my defender, my protector, my ally, and friend.

Sometimes I relive the moments and then for others like now I stand before you and collect the precious memories. I see you... I hear you... I feel my essence touch you and I smile...

And I smile... And I smile.

166

With Respect

In tears of sorrow do I mourn my yesterdays gone as I walk the avenues of my mind and rebuild the pictures of my life, frame by frame.

Detail by detail I keep recollecting until the picture is complete and I am completely aware of who I am... what I am... and where I come from...

I keep remembering and building until each moment is so distinct that it's captured in time, my living legacy.

Or, as I replay each reel I see you sitting within life shadows and then within its light teaching about life rules, life values and life's ethics.

In speech I hear the texture of your intellect from its tone, and in your writing as you weave each word, each phrase, each line into a sentence it is so obvious that you are inspirational, and worthy of respect.

So with respect I tell you that the tears we cry are the raindrops that nourish our parched dry soul.

And our smiles, our laughter and our friendship are after all life's golden sunshine.

I tell you that because of you my life is richer, my days are more promising and that you are a great part of my life lessons.

As my teacher you have allowed me the ability to grow and aspire to reach for my dreams.

You allow me to be a better son, a better daughter, a better sister or a better brother and your guidance and wisdom is beyond compare.

I look at you and see your grace, your style and it is obvious, so obvious that you are an exotic flower that blooms rarely.

As my friend you have taught me that true friendship is an eternal bond that will absorb the shocks and knocks that life delivers.

That true friendship can and does get dirty yet when put to the test its core is still pure and that discretion is still the better part of valor.

Whereas, honor and respect is the cup from which we draw its sustenance.

Once, yes long ago I thought that to be free was the ultimate quest that I should seek.

I defined being free as strength, no worries, and within the boundaries I set.

I thought that to be strong I had to control my emotions and the things around me.

167

I thought... And then I realized that in life there is no concept that is totally free, I realize that my freedom was simply an expanded box of my own choosing.

I realized that freedom is a thought or an idea that is but a fleeting mirage seen that entices the senses and help us to dream and achieve.

I realized that with respect life is the ultimate symbol of freedom and with the people we have around us, the people we meet our family, our friends our box expands and so does the term free.

Two Hearts

They say that heavens rewards are magnificent and beyond measure.
They say that they are our stolen moments in time, the captured dreams we thought would pass us by our trials and our journeys.
This journey... When first I asked you to walk this path with me I never dreamed or expected that our road would bend so much or twist and turn.
I didn't fully understand that sometime even the best of times would challenge our commitment, our patience or our love.
I didn't understand.
But, I knew that at the worst of times our love would rise to the challenges that we faced and that it would give us the strength we needed.
I knew that for the times that I fell down you would lift me up, when I leaned too far to the right or the left you would be my shoulder to lean on and in the middle of the night when I wanted to cry my tears it would be okay because you would be the one to hold me.
In my dreams I knew.
You see in dreams do we plot the course of our lives, plan for the trials we believe we shall face, anticipate those we can't define and pray.
If I had known long ago that I could look forward in time to this moment and that it would be such a defining moment of our lives together then, I would have prayed harder anticipated more and dreamed every day of my life.
If I had known that our casual meeting, that our first date, our first walk together, our first kiss, our first movie and long talks would lead to this! Twenty years later...
I would have fallen upon my knees and prayed to God in heaven and asked him to touch our souls and unite them, and to baptize our soul in his holy spirit.
If? I had known.
That in dreams I could travel through time and foresee this moment and the passage of times flight I would have as the saying goes moved heaven and earth to let you view the dream through my eyes.
Or: if? I had known how to step outside of myself and put you into this body of mine to let you feel the true depth of my love. I would...

If I could reach up and catch a shooting star my wish would be that our two hearts continue as one and that our soul's march side by side down through the years as we age gracefully.

It would be that God's grace would wash us clean and seal us within his love as we do our twenty years to life.

It would be that our two hearts, our two minds continue, as one will together.

It would be that our two hearts remain as one love all encompassing of God.

Because... We are two hearts, one dream, on one path walking together in faith of God.

We are two hearts and blessed beyond measure...

Autobiography

Who am I?

Well that is simple I am the son of Essie Mae and Junior Lee Green, and I am the Intimate Trilogy. I am the eighth child of ten born and raised in Quincy, Florida.

What am I?

Why! I am the words that I have written. I am a poet aspiring to write the tales of my life; my thoughts, my desires, and my values. This book talks about my faith and my experiences it talks about my role models and in part it is who I am. It is respect and love and it represents me each page, each paragraph, every line sentence and word. There are no false accolades, no titles just me; read it and believe. Hear me… Feel me… Welcome and enjoy the journey.

CPSIA information can be obtained at www.ICGtesting.com
Printed in the USA
LVOW01s1138201213

365892LV00008B/292/P